LOUIS XIV
OF FRANCE

King Louis XIV of France (1638–1715), by Hyacinthe Rigaud.
Louvre, Paris.

IMMORTALS OF HISTORY

LOUIS XIV
OF FRANCE
Pattern of Majesty

BY MONROE STEARNS

FRANKLIN WATTS, INC.
845 Third Avenue, New York, N.Y. 10022

No man can be fully known, in soul and spirit and mind, until he has been seen versed in rule and law-giving.

Sophocles, *Antigone*

All photographs except those on pages 47, 75, and 135, courtesy the French Embassy Press & Information Division.

SBN 531–00962–9
Library of Congress Catalog Card Number: 77-137152
Copyright © 1971 by Franklin Watts, Inc.
Printed in the United States of America

1 2 3 4 5 6

CONTENTS

Inset map (top left):

NORTH SEA

UNITED PROVINCES

Amsterdam

The Hague • Ryswick • Utrecht
Nijmegen

ZEELAND

Rhine

Bruges • Ghent • Antwerp
Menin • Brussels • Brühl • Cologne
Oudenaarde • Neerwinden • Aix-la-Chapelle
Lille • Ramillies • Liège
Lens • Mons • Namur
Arras • Malplaquet
Denain

SPANISH NETHERLANDS

FRANCE

Rocroi

LUXEMBOURG

• Rheims

BUCEL

Miles
0   50   100

SCOTLAND

Top right panel:

WESTERN EUROPE
17th Century

Main map:

NORWAY

SWEDEN

DENMARK

BALTIC SEA

BRANDENBURG (PRUSSIA)

NORTH SEA

IRELAND

Boyne R.

ENGLAND
London •

Beachy Head

ENGLISH CHANNEL

UNITED PROVINCES

Rhine

WESTPHALIA

SP. NETHERLANDS

RHENISH PALATINATE

THE HOLY ROMAN EMPIRE

ATLANTIC OCEAN

Le Havre • Rocroi
Seine R. • Rheims
Versailles • Paris

Philippsburg • Blenheim • Ratisbon
Strasbourg • BAVARIA • AUSTRIA
Augsburg • Vienna

Nantes •

Loire R.

FRANCHE COMTÉ

Radstadt •

FRANCE

SWITZERLAND

La Rochelle •

ALPS

Lyons •

VENETIAN REPUBLIC

BAY OF BISCAY

Bordeaux •

SAVOY
Pinerolo • Turin • Milan • Casale • Parma • Modena

Rhone R.

Avignon •

GENOA

TUSCANY

PAPAL STATES

Fuentarrabia •

PYRENEES

Marseilles •

CORSICA

Rome •

KINGDOM OF NAPLES AND TWO SICILIES

PORTUGAL

CATALONIA

Barcelona •

Naples •

Madrid •

SPAIN

SARDINIA

Valencia •

Almanza •

MEDITERRANEAN SEA

Miles
0   100   200   300

• Malaga
• Gibraltar

SICILY

LOUIS XIV TODAY

Historians tend to judge the stature of a head of state in terms of what he set as political objectives—domestic and external—for his country and to what degree he achieved them. By that standard of judgment, King Louis XIV of France (1638–1715) deserves his reputation as one of the greatest rulers of modern times. Indeed, since he dominated his own world, his reign is often said to mark the beginning of modern history, for the course of events since his death has been either a continuation of his method of government or a reaction against it.

That method depended upon a policy of absolutism, militarism, and nationalism. Its effectiveness demanded intolerance and censorship. It put the welfare of the state before consideration of any segment of the population or of the individual citizen's freedom. In those respects it was similar to the governments of about half the people of today's world. The governments of the other half represent a moral challenge to such policies which has sometimes become an active resistance to them.

The citizens of that half of today's world which calls itself free find it hard, therefore, to consider Louis XIV great.

It is not unusual for them to compare him to Adolf Hitler. And it is hard to deny that Louis XIV's methods of government produced not a happy, prosperous people, but an impoverished and discontented nation.

The analogy, however, leaves out of account at least one supremely important factor. Hitler beguiled a sick-spirited nation with lies, whereas Louis XIV inspired a healthy-spirited people with a vision of glory. Furthermore, egocentric as Louis XIV was, he could nevertheless subordinate his own inclinations to the welfare of his country. That welfare always meant to Louis XIV the fulfillment of his nation's potential. For that goal he sacrificed personal happiness and also humbled himself to the sense of history. Consequently, when he asked the French people for their loyalty, they gave it to him willingly and enthusiastically. No small aspect of his greatness was his efficient use of the national spirit.

Louis XIV's deeds, good or bad, are almost as forgotten today as those of the pharaohs of ancient Egypt. Like those mighty monarchs he is remembered chiefly by the monuments he left. They serve to remind the people of France of the glory he made their national heritage.

LOUIS XIV
OF FRANCE

Saint-Germain
Rueil
Marly
Saint-Cyr
Versailles
Port Royal
Meudon
PARIS
Louvre
Vincennes
Charenton
Seine River
BIÈVRE

Miles
0   5

FRANCE

ENGLAND
NORTH SEA
NETHERLANDS
Dunkirk
FLANDERS
Lille
Brussels
BELGIUM
Arras
GERMANY
Rhine R.
Beachy Head
ENGLISH CHANNEL
Dieppe
Péronne
St-Quentin
Rocroi
Rheims
LUXEMBOURG
Luxembourg
La Hogue
Le Havre
Seine R.
Chantilly
LORRAINE
NORMANDY
Versailles
Chevreuse
Maintenon
Chartres
Paris
Melun
Fontainebleau
Strasbourg
ALSACE
BLACK FOREST
Belle-Isle
BRITTANY
Orleans
Vendôme
Bellegarde
Bléneau
Chambord
BURGUNDY
FRANCHE-COMTÉ
SWITZ.
Nantes
Loire River
Poitiers
ATLANTIC OCEAN
La Rochelle
Brouage
F R A N C E
Lyons
Grenoble
ITALY
BAY OF BISCAY
Bordeaux
G U Y E N N E
Garonne River
Rhône River
Alais
Nîmes
Avignon
Marseilles
Toulon
Fuentarrabia
ISLE OF PHEASANTS
Bidassoa R.
St-Jean-de-Luz
ANDORRA
S P A I N
CATALONIA
MEDITERRANEAN SEA

Miles
0   50   100   150

I

THE CHILDHOOD OF A GOD

Anne of Austria, queen of Louis XIII, the second Bourbon king of France, was considerably surprised on the rainy evening of December 5, 1637, by the arrival in her apartments in the Louvre palace in Paris of the captain of her husband's guards. This Captain Guitaut besought her to advance her customary late supper hour, for, as he explained, the king was eager to share her board.

Guitaut undoubtedly did not add that he hoped the king would also share her bed, but such was very much on the captain's mind. Nor did he say that he had persuaded the king to spend the night in Paris rather than drag his exhausted suite of attendants through the cold, stormy darkness on a twelve-mile ride back to Versailles. And surely Guitaut did not tell the queen that the king was in the city he disliked only to visit his dear friend Mlle de La Fayette, at whose convent* in Paris's Rue Saint-Antoine he had been trapped by the raging downpour.

Guitaut saw to it that the queen's menu was altered to

* A convent then frequently served as a supervised residence for a noblewoman who wished, or had, to retire from court life. Cardinal Richelieu, Louis XIII's prime minister, had ordered Mlle de La Fayette to withdraw to one.

3

suit the king's taste and that everything else was arranged to please His Majesty. When it appeared that Louis XIII would indeed spend the night with the woman whom politics had forced upon him as a wife twenty-two years earlier, Captain Guitaut sent a messenger to all the religious houses in Paris to entreat their prayers that the long-awaited heir to the throne of France might result from this reconciliation between the royal pair who had been estranged for seventeen years.

Anne prayed too. The king's neglect had saddened her as a woman and prevented her from fulfilling her chief obligation to France, which was to provide an heir to the throne in the direct line of the House of Bourbon. Her double disappointment had driven her into a frivolous social life. That had involved her with the Duke of Buckingham in the scandalous affair of the "Diamond Necklace."* The result was that she had become so antagonistic to Louis XIII's policies and ministers that many persons in the government suspected her of disloyalty to the kingdom. To counteract that suspicion, the beautiful, passionate, Spanish-bred queen** exchanged some of her dedication to gambling, dancing, and the theater for devotion to religion in the hope that she might bear the king a son.

On the morning of December 6, a Franciscan friar told the queen that he had had a vision that her prayers would be answered. And on January 20, 1638, the *Gazette*† pub-

---

* This intrigue forms the principal plot of Alexander Dumas's famous cloak-and-sword novel, *The Three Musketeers.*

** In spite of her title, "Anne of Austria," Louis XIII's queen was actually a Spaniard, the daughter of King Philip III of Spain, who was of the Austrian Hapsburg family, which ruled the Holy Roman Empire. Spain had been separated from that Empire in 1556, but it continued to be ruled by a branch of the Hapsburg family, which had adopted Spanish traditions.

† *La Gazette*, France's first newspaper, had been founded by Théophraste Renaudot in 1631.

lished the startling news that the queen was pregnant. On February 10, King Louis XIII dedicated his crown and his kingdom to the Blessed Virgin in the fervent hope that the child would be a boy. Anne herself vowed to erect a church* in honor of the Virgin if the Mother of God granted her prayer for a son.

On August 28, 1638, Queen Anne felt her time approaching. Public prayers for her safe delivery began throughout the kingdom. The royal family and the whole court hastened to the palace of Saint-Germain, thirteen miles northwest of Paris, for the doctors, with an inaccuracy typical of their profession in those times, predicted August 31 as the fateful date. It was not, however, until eleven thirty on the morning of Sunday, September 5, that Mme Péronne, the midwife, joyfully shouted that a male child had been born to the royal couple.

The infant was immediately named Louis le Dieudonné (the gift of God), for everyone in France knew that the prayers of the king and queen and of every loyal Frenchman had been answered.

The king fell on his knees to give thanks for the miracle, but he had to be urged to go to his wife's bedside and thank her with a kiss.

By that time fifty couriers had been dispatched to carry the glad tidings throughout the realm. The cannons were booming, and the bells ringing. Huge casks of wine were broached in the squares so that the people could drink to their future king, and in every church *Te Deums* were sung and masses offered for the survival of the dauphin (the traditional

---

* This beautiful chapel of Val-de-Grace, 277 Rue Saint-Jacques, Paris, was built between 1645 and 1665 by François Mansard and Jacques Lemercier. It is one of the most typical and best examples of the architecture of the period of Louis XIV.

title of an heir to the French throne). For two days bonfires, street dancing, fireworks, band concerts, and parades with floats filled every street in Paris—and, as the news arrived, in every other town up to the borders of France.

The baby was given over to the care of the Marquise de Lansac, whom the king had appointed governess of the royal children. Little Louis had been merely sprinkled with holy water by the bishop of Meaux; his formal baptism would not take place until Louis XIII lay dying.

Anne of Austria, however, devoted herself entirely to the guidance of the son who had not only completed her life as a woman and a queen, but had restored her to the confidence of the French people. The love that she could not give her husband—even after the birth of the dauphin their relations continued very cool—she lavished on her first child. She was a mature woman now, and as sensible as her limited intelligence permitted. The young prince profited from her genuine affection, which, as he himself matured he fully returned.

Louis XIII, on the other hand, was envious of the beautiful baby—the chief topic of conversation at the court—and jealous of his wife's attentions to the child. The king was of a gloomy temperament anyway, and his personality was cold and stern. It is small wonder that the child was terrified of him and hid behind his mother's skirts whenever the king found time to visit the nursery.

Such behavior infuriated Louis XIII. He blamed Anne for it and threatened to remove his son from her supervision. Probably the queen and the governess worked on the child to be more demonstrative toward his father, for by the time the dauphin was eighteen months old, Louis XIII could write to his prime minister, Cardinal Richelieu: ". . . my son asked my forgiveness on his knees, and played with me for a whole hour.

King Louis XIII of France (1601–43), father of Louis XIV.
Anne of Austria, queen of France (1601–66), mother of Louis XIV.

I gave him some toys, and we are the best of friends. I pray God it may last."

The king's nineteen-year-old favorite, Henri de Ruzé, Marquis de Cinq-Mars, thought that better relations between Louis XIII and Anne of Austria might be to his own advantage. Possibly due to Cinq-Mars's influence, Louis XIII spent Christmas Eve of 1639 with his wife. On January 28, 1640, the *Gazette* announced that Her Majesty again was pregnant. On September 21, she gave birth to another son, who was named Philippe and was created Duc d'Anjou. (Later, on the death of his uncle Gaston, who had no sons, only daughters, he became Duc d'Orléans, and was given the court title of "Monsieur.")

The succession to the throne was now well assured to the direct Bourbon line.

Anne was determined that Philippe would never be a menace to Louis; the brother of a king could often be a threat to the monarch in those days of plots and palace intrigues. Consequently she brought Philippe up as if he were a girl. As a result, he became an effeminate and corrupt man, though not lacking in physical bravery. Louis was fond of his brother, but, like their mother, kept him subordinate and gave him no important responsibilities.

Philippe meant no more to his father emotionally than Louis did. King Louis XIII was too occupied with his hunting dogs and his horses to give his sons much time. Since he preferred the rough masculine society of his own sporting court to the refined language and the atmosphere of culture that the educated women of Paris (*les précieuses*) were introducing into the court of the queen, he continued to spend most of his time at his hunting lodge in Versailles.

For twenty years Louis XIII had suffered from tuberculosis. His health completely gave way under the shock of the trial and execution of Cinq-Mars. That favorite of his had conspired with the king's brother, Gaston, Duc d'Orléans, and other high nobles to assassinate Cardinal Richelieu on September 12, 1642. Another shock to the king was the death—from natural causes—of Richelieu on December 4.

There was a myth that Louis XIII could not govern without that great statesman, but the fact was that the king was a hardworking, conscientious administrator, intelligent, watchful, and brave. He always maintained his right to veto Richelieu's measures and exercised it in favor of the rights and traditions of his subjects, which Richelieu often tried to suppress. For this reason he was known as Louis the Just and was regarded as almost as great a king—though never so beloved—as his father, Henry IV, the heroic Henry of Navarre.

On February 21, 1643, Louis XIII took to his bed at Saint-Germain for the last time. The king spent his final days on earth in an effort to ensure a peaceful transmission of the crown to his elder son, who was now four and one-half years old. His effort culminated in the formal baptism of Louis by the bishop of Meaux in the chapel of the château of Saint-Germain on April 21, 1643.

The dauphin's godmother was Charlotte Montmorency, Princesse de Condé. Thirty-four years earlier, when she was sixteen years old, she had caught the eye of his fifty-six-year-old grandfather, Henri IV, and thereby had almost started a general European war. His godfather was perhaps a wiser choice—Cardinal Jules Mazarin (born Giulio Mazarini), who had neatly stepped into Cardinal Richelieu's shoes as prime minister.

An often-told story is that, after the ceremony, Louis came in his cloth-of-gold baptismal gown to the bedside of his dying father.

"What is your name?" asked the king.

"Louis XIV."

"Not yet," replied the jealous father. "Not yet."

Then Louis XIII prayed that his son might have the grace to reign in peace as a true Christian. Three weeks later he died, at two thirty in the afternoon of May 14, without having made up with his wife.

Another much-repeated story is that Louis—now truly Louis XIV—wept and shrieked that he would rather throw himself into the palace moat than be king. Probably, however, he felt little emotion. He rarely spoke of his father—and almost never of Cardinal Richelieu. If anything, he doubtless thought that the world was well rid of those two men, who had treated his beloved mother so cruelly. Any grief he may have felt was dispelled by the excitement of preparing for his first appearance before the Parlement of Paris* on May 18.

By that day, Queen Anne had bustled her children from Saint-Germain into Paris, for the Bourbons never remained under the same roof with a corpse. The citizens of the French capital were delighted with their handsome, blond, serious-eyed child king. They had always admired the queen's looks. She was still beautiful in face and figure, and her hands were famous for their exquisite shape and grace.

Cardinal Mazarin had seen to it that there would be no opposition in Parlement to the revisions he had made in Louis XIII's will. That document, actually worthless insofar as the disposition of power was concerned, had named Gaston d'Orléans regent of France during Louis XIV's minority. Mazarin promised Parlement that there would be no more of the friction it had experienced with Louis XIII and Richelieu if it named Anne of Austria as regent. The cardinal assured the queen that Parlement would ratify her claim to be the sole guardian of her son and would grant her "full power and freedom" to govern his kingdom for him.

* The Parlement (not to be confused with a parliament in the English sense of that institution as a representative lawmaking body) was a final court of appeals. Its members were lawyers. Each of them had bought his seat from the king, and could hold it for life unless the king could manage to repurchase it. Parlement registered the king's edicts if it found them acceptable to the law of the land. The king, however, could overrule an adverse decision by appearing in person and thus constituting a session of Parlement known as a *lit de justice* (bed of justice)—so called from the custom of early French kings hearing cases while sitting on a couch. Often the king bribed members of Parlement to follow his wishes. Parlement also administered certain laws. There were Parlements in other major cities in France, but the Parlement of Paris was the most important. It met in a building adjacent to the Sainte-Chapelle, now reconstructed into the Palais de Justice, on the Ile de la Cité.

Omer Talon, a leader of Parlement and its spokesman, addressed the king, who was still wearing dresses, and eloquently impressed upon him the duty of a monarch. Talon urged the boy to follow the examples of his merciful grandfather and his righteous father.

"Sire," Talon said, "Your Majesty's position represents to us the throne of the living God. The people of France of all ranks and orders pay you honor and reverence as to a visible deity. . . . Be, Sire," he concluded, "the father of your people, so that in their deep misery they may find comfort in you. Give France what is more valuable than victories. Strive to be the prince of peace."

Talon's last remarks proved to be an ironic prophecy. On the day after that *lit de justice*, the king's twenty-two-year-old cousin, Louis II de Bourbon (then the Duc d'Enghien, but later to be known as the Great Condé), won for France a decisive victory over Spain at Rocroi in the Ardennes on the border of Luxembourg. A month later began five years of negotiations for a treaty to end the ghastly Thirty Years' War. For the time being, Louis XIV seemed indeed to be a "prince of peace."

The next seventy years, however, would show that he could also be described as the captain of the Four Horsemen of the Apocalypse—conquest, war, famine, and death. A more accurate prophecy was made by the Dutch scholar and statesman Hugo Grotius, later Sweden's ambassador to France. When he learned that Louis XIV had been born with two front teeth which caused his wet nurses much pain, he wrote to the king of Sweden: "The dauphin is not content to milk his nurses dry, but bites them to pieces. France's neighbors should fear this precocious voracity."

The earlier tribute of the realistic Omer Talon was perhaps intended merely as the flattery customarily offered a sovereign, but the young king and his mother believed it implicitly. Talon's words, moreover, reflected the universal attitude of the French toward their ruler—that he was the visible symbol of an omnipotent God directly concerned with the course of human events. The seventeenth-century historian André Duchesne had put this belief into a formula: "The kings of France are so pleasing to God that He chose them to become His lieutenants upon earth."

To about twenty million Frenchmen, therefore, the worship of God involved a worship of their king. To disobey, or even to question, a king's will was considered a sin equal to blasphemy. The theologians of the time propounded and defended the theory that a divinely appointed monarch was the highest possible form of human government. It was as much a duty of the French people to accept this dogma as to believe in the Trinity and the Virgin Birth. If Louis XIV himself ever faltered in that belief—and he never did—he would have been forcibly reminded of it by his spiritual advisers. Jacques Bossuet, the foremost preacher of the age, thundered to him on Palm Sunday, 1662: "*Vous êtes Dieu*" ("You are God").

Louis XIV would write for the benefit of his own son: "However bad the king may be, the revolt of his subjects is always criminal. He [God] who has given kings to men has required that they should be respected as His lieutenants, reserving to Himself alone the right to examine their conduct. It is His will that he who is born a subject should obey without question."*

---

* From the *Mémoires* of Louis XIV, composed for the instruction in kingship of his eldest son. They were probably written by one or another of Louis's secretaries, perhaps at his dictation or from his notes, and perhaps as a paraphrase of what he said from time to time or as a compendium of what the writers felt he believed. At any rate, Louis XIV acknowledged them as a true presentation of his principles. They

That arrogantly self-confident statement of absolutism, so abhorrent to twentieth-century political thought, nevertheless involves the òbligations of an absolute monarch to the absolute power that has placed him on the throne. Absolutism is not necessarily totalitarianism. Much of the greatness of Louis XIV is due to his confining himself to actions within the framework of custom and the common good—what might be called the common law of his realm if that term had had any significance in seventeenth-century France. The phrase, "the needs of the state," occurs frequently in Louis XIV's *Mémoires* as an explanation or justification of his measures. To that phrase, however, should be added "as the king saw those needs."

Strange as these beliefs may seem to the mid-twentieth-century American, they were nonetheless a "fact" of existence in seventeenth-century France. The irony is that while France under Louis XIV was in many respects the most civilized nation in the world, its political theory was still that of a primitive society. Other nations at the same time, notably England, were far more politically advanced. But the baby doll of a king who was presented to the Parlement of Paris on May 18, 1643, was, even to the learned, worldly jurists of that august body, the fetish of their tribe. That fact must be accepted by the reader—perhaps with a willing suspension of disbelief—or the history of the period and of Louis XIV himself appears a preposterous farce.

Anne of Austria, now the nominal ruler of France, determined to be the real director of her royal son's education. Her limited intelligence simplified that process into two vague

---

contain a narrative of his reign from 1661 to 1668, and also letters up to 1693. Louis's principal secretary during those years was Paul Pellisson; another was Toussaint Rose, who could copy the king's handwriting and signature with absolute accuracy.

principles: Louis was to be a "good man" and a great king. To make sure that her control was not jeopardized by a governess who had been thrust upon her by Louis XIII, Anne dismissed Mme de Lansac, and replaced her with Mme de Sénecé, who had been a girlhood friend and companion. Further to demonstrate her independence, the queen moved her household, on October 7, 1643, from the traditional Louvre palace, old and full of unhappy memories, to the newer Palais-Royal, which Richelieu had completed in 1636 and then bequeathed to Louis XIII. This was to be the childhood home of Louis XIV.

The queen entrusted the supervision of the boy king to the servants of her ladies-in-waiting, and to the servants of those servants. Hence, Louis's earliest companions were chambermaids, valets, and guards. The last amused him most; he soon learned from them how to beat a drum, handle a toy sword, and bark out commands. He loved playing captain to his "soldier" playmates and drilling them. France had been engaged in the Thirty Years' War since before Louis's birth, and as that conflict was not yet ended, military matters dominated the talk of the lower levels of the royal household.

The domestics were often too busy about their primary duties to keep close watch over the active little boy. Once he fell into a fountain and almost drowned before someone pulled him out. His everyday clothes were ragged and dirty, and he outgrew them before they were replaced. His dressing gown, the common warm garment for informal wear in the freezing rooms of those times, was supposed to reach the floor, but finally it hung above his knees. There was not much money allotted to maintaining his establishment.

When Louis was seven years old, his education was handed over from women to men. His new superintendent was the forty-seven-year-old soldier, Nicolas de Villeroi, who was so devout a believer in the cult of the king-god that he never denied his young charge anything. After all, how could a mere mortal argue with the god-inspired wishes of a French king? Consequently Louis nicknamed his governor "Monsieur Oui-sire" from Villeroi's habitual answer, *"Oui, Sire"* ("Yes, Sire.") It is, therefore, not surprising that Louis learned and did only what he pleased.

Anne of Austria was now too concerned with the duties and functions of regency to play with her children as she used to do when they were babies. Her sons saw her only at her formal rising from bed, at about eleven in the morning, and during her breakfast of soup, chops, and sausages. Then Louis was permitted the honor of handing his mother her gown, kissing her, and watching her being dressed. After that ceremony, Anne left on her continuous round of court appointments and entertainments.

Anne's way of accomplishing her intention that Louis be a "good man" was to take him with her on her frequent visits to churches, chapels, and shrines. There they listened to sermons that urged the king to protect the church and destroy heresy. The ritual-observing regent saw to it that her son was punished by being confined to his room if he was disobedient and if he used foul language. That was her conception of the Christian life, the pursuit of which would automatically make one a "good man."

Louis observed the forms and practices of religion all his life, but it is doubtful that he had much understanding of what religion is all about. His first cousin, La Grande Mademoiselle,* complained that he had never even read the Bible.

Louis was not himself much of a reader; instead, his tutors

---

*Anne Marie Louise d'Orléans, Duchesse de Montpensier, daughter of Gaston d'Orléans and Marie de Bourbon. She was the richest woman in France.

read to him. The only book he is known to have read was Julius Caesar's *Commentaries*, for he translated Book One of them. (The translation was published in 1651.) That autobiographical piece of political propaganda would have interested him because it was about war and because it was an easy way for him to learn Latin, then the universal language of politics and diplomacy. He later spent many hours improving his mastery of Latin.

Louis's head tutor was Hardouin de Péréfixe, bishop of Rodez and later archbishop of Paris, who had written an idealized history of the reign of Henry IV. Louis never let the heroic image of his grandfather grow dim, even when court gossip and the presence of Henry IV's illegitimate children revealed the less admirable traits of that ruler's character. From Péréfixe, Louis learned the value to a king of decisive action, and also the maxim he later passed on to his son as his own: "A king should take pleasure in his calling."

Since Louis's writing master set him to copying such pleasant sentences as "Homage is due to kings; they do what they please," it was not hard for him to become rather priggish. The wonder is that he was not more so.

He learned a little Spanish and a little Italian, some mathematics and some geography, but his notions of history were derived from listening to his valet, Pierre de La Porte, read him to sleep from François de Mézeray's history of France, the first volume of which was published in 1643. (It is, unfortunately, only the later volumes which are truly good history; those were not published until the king was too busy or too indifferent to read them himself.)

A touching story of the lack of true affection Louis suffered is La Porte's account of how the lonely little boy would crawl into bed with his valet for comfort and security. Perhaps Louis resented his mother's intimacy with Cardinal

Mazarin. Perhaps he felt himself less popular than his brother; Philippe was a cheerful child, whereas no one ever saw Louis laugh. There was a childish rivalry between the two brothers.

Louis, however, had plenty of other playmates. These were chosen for him from among the children of the nobility. Their favorite game was attacking or defending a model fort in the garden of the Palais-Royal. There were also swimming parties—if indeed anyone could swim in the bathing suits the boys were compelled to wear. The group was trained in muscle-building exercises and in horseback riding; they also learned to use a sword and a spear, to shoot, to hunt, and to dance. Louis became an excellent shot, and he always adored hunting and dancing.

In the summer of his eighth year, 1647, Louis went with his mother and Cardinal Mazarin to raise the morale of the French soldiers who were fighting on the frontier of the Spanish Netherlands (present-day Belgium). In spite of the peace conference in session, the Thirty Years' War still continued. It was a disappointing campaign for the French, marked by mutinies both on that front and in Spain. The experience was a sobering lesson to Louis that real war is considerably different from games around a toy fort, even in a time when war was still enough of a gentleman's game for the defender of a town to send lemonade every morning to the besieger. The only real pleasure the boy king got from the trip was a visit to the port of Dieppe—his first glimpse of the sea. There he took part in a sham naval battle in which, of course, his side won.

On November 10, 1647, Louis fell a victim to smallpox, a scourge of high and low alike, which only about fifty percent of its victims survived. It was two weeks before the fever broke and the king, who had been in a coma, began to recover. When he appeared at court on Christmas Day, his childish beauty was gone. For the rest of his days he carried the marks of the disease on his face.

The following January 15, Louis had to appear in Parlement again. A *lit de justice* was necessary because the members of Parlement had refused to register a burdensome new tax law. The war and a bad harvest had reduced the country to misery, and more money was needed to extract a victory after the disastrous campaigns of 1647. The poor people of Paris clung to the royal carriage, beseeching help, as it conveyed the king to the Palais de Justice.

The tone of this session of Parlement was considerably different from that of Louis's first *lit de justice*. Omer Talon reminded him now of his duty to keep his subjects free men, not slaves. He appealed to Louis's pride as a sovereign and to the queen regent's conscience, demanding their pity for the suffering people whom "conquered provinces cannot nourish and who have no bread and do not value palms and laurels as they do the produce of their lands."

A wiser ruler than Anne of Austria might have heeded the warning of Parlement, for its members, although not elected by the people, represented the people's way of thinking. Anne, however, like many other rulers of her time, had no more feeling for the people than for a flock of poultry. When she returned from the *lit de justice* to her palace, she wept out of sheer rage at Parlement's insolence.

But the nine-year-old king had come face-to-face with a force that would not "*Oui, Sire*" him automatically. Perhaps he recognized even then that weeping with rage was not the best way of combating it.

II

THE CARDINAL'S PUPIL

The target of Parlement's opposition to the measures of the regency was Cardinal Jules Mazarin. It was he who initiated all governmental policy. Anne of Austria merely rubber-stamped the proposals of her minister, for whom she had such a great fondness and respect that it has been thought they were married.

Their marriage would have been possible. Although a cardinal, Mazarin had never taken final holy orders. As a young man, he was too fond of the pleasures of this world to become a priest after he finished his education at a Jesuit college. The son of a poor but ambitious father who was the head steward, or household manager, of the constable of Naples, he took to gambling to get the money he needed to pursue those pleasures—and was extremely successful at the gaming tables in his native Italy and later in Spain, where he went as valet to the constable's son, Girolamo Colonna, supposedly to study law.

Law interested the handsome, witty, intelligent twenty-year-old Giulio Mazarini far less than did the society of cosmopolitan Madrid. Soon he had fallen in love with the daughter

of a notary from whom he had borrowed money to recoup
his losses at cards. Girolamo Colonna disapproved of this
romance and sent his valet back to Italy, where Constable
Filippo Colonna dismissed him with a vigorous scolding.

Mazarini then joined the papal army, from which he took
French leave to visit his sick mother. Threatened with court-
martial, he appealed to Pope Urban VIII, whom he so impressed that the pontiff made him secretary to the ineffectual
Cardinal Antonio Barberini. Barberini was to negotiate terms
with Cardinal Richelieu that would keep the French army
from invading Italy.

Captain Mazarini talked for three solid hours at the conference in Lyons, France, on January 29, 1630, but he failed
to achieve a truce. He did not fail, however, to impress
Richelieu, who invited him to dinner. Five months later, at
another inconclusive conference in Grenoble, Richelieu in-
troduced Mazarini to King Louis XIII. Finally, in October,
1630, when the French were besieging Casale in Italy, Mazarini
suddenly appeared between the French and the papal armies,
shouting: "Peace! Peace!" That daring gesture got him the
truce he wanted. The pope rewarded him by making him a
canon, and for a while Monsignor Mazarini was the most
popular man in Europe.

When Richelieu's trusted adviser and diplomatic agent,
Père Joseph du Tremblay—the man whose shadowy influence
on world history made his nickname, *l'Eminence Grise* (the
gray—that is, unobtrusive—cardinal), a byword in all languages
—died in 1638, Richelieu approached Monsignor Giulio Mazarini to replace him. Mazarini agreed. On December 14, 1639,
he deserted the pope's service in Rome and moved permanently
to Paris. He changed his name to Jules Mazarin, but he never
became a naturalized Frenchman.

As a reward for his services to the French prime minister,

Cardinal Jules Mazarin (1602–61).

Louis XIII got the pope to make Mazarin a cardinal on December 16, 1641, and himself gave him the cardinal's hat the following February. On the day after Richelieu died, Louis XIII admitted Cardinal Mazarin to the council of state in reward, as the king said, "for his numerous faithful services which have made us trust him as much as if he had been born our subject."

Mazarin had learned an enormous amount about statecraft from Richelieu, who was the most dreaded statesman in Europe. The two men, however, were different in personality, and each used different methods. Richelieu, a Frenchman, was direct, rigid, forceful, and cruel, never hesitating to imprison, exile, or execute an opponent. Mazarin, an Italian, said of himself: "I dissemble, I am evasive, I pacify. I compromise—just as much as I possibly can" in order to achieve the good of the state.

That suppleness of character made it difficult for the solid, straightforward—and self-interested—members of Parlement to understand and to cope with the regent's prime minister. They also despised Mazarin because of his comic-opera career, which had culminated with his insinuating himself into Louis XIII's favor. (Richelieu had shrewdly advised the king merely to use Mazarin, not to give him power.) Most of all, they hated Mazarin for being an Italian. As a foreigner, they believed, he could never truly understand and gratify the needs of Frenchmen.

In that last respect, the Parlementaires of Paris, who regarded themselves as the city fathers, may have been right. Mazarin lacked Richelieu's ability to assess the temper of the people. He moved to suppress Parlement's opposition with measures that the members saw would reduce their prestige and—worse yet—empty their pockets.

On July 12, 1648, Parlement responded with a document

that was essentially a constitution for a limited monarchy. They presented this at a session to which they had summoned the other law courts. The regent and her son also attended it. Louis, therefore, heard many arguments in favor of a democracy, such as "it is not kings who make the kingdom, but rather the multitude." He must have wondered how true his copybook maxim was that kings can do whatever they please.

In order to gain time so that he might appear to lead from strength, Mazarin subtly appeared to agree to the twenty-seven articles of the republican document. He communicated to the Prince de Condé, who as Duc d'Enghien had won the battle of Rocroi, that a victory in the war was essential. The reason was that the law that Mazarin needed to have ratified by Parlement was to raise taxes for the continuation of the war with Spain and Austria which was still going against France. Condé obliged with a smashing defeat of the Spaniards at Lens in the Spanish Netherlands on August 20.

Louis XIV, who naturally sided with his mother and godfather, remarked in reference to the victory: "The gentlemen of Parlement are going to be very unhappy about this."

Having drawn the cards he wanted, Mazarin ordered the arrest, on August 25, of the elderly Pierre Broussel, a member of Parlement who had become a demagogue by his shouting to the already overtaxed people, "No more taxes!" Three other members were arrested with him.

The next day a mob gathered at the Palais-Royal to demand their release. The queen declared that she would rather strangle Broussel with her own hands than have him freed. Barricades of benches, chains, and paving stones went up in the streets of Paris to defend the rebellious citizens from the royal troops. The mob was yelling "Long live the king! Death to Mazarin!" and slinging stones at the soldiers who were attempting to suppress them. Hence the rebels were called *frondeurs* (sling-ers), and the party of Parlement, the *Fronde*.

The queen believed that for her to yield to the 160 members of Parlement who came to petition her would be to betray the rights of her son. Mazarin, however, advised her to give in, and she did have Broussel released from prison. Anne and Louis then fled from the mobs to Richelieu's old residence in the suburb of Rueil. On October 22, Mazarin granted Parle-ment's demands, but the barricades remained in the streets until he should enforce the new legislation.

Mazarin delayed enforcing the articles. Instead, he in-structed his agent at the peace conference in Westphalia to conclude the negotiations at once. Thanks to the French victory at Lens, he could get good terms for France. The treaties were signed on October 24, 1648. The Thirty Years' War was over at last. Then Mazarin summoned Condé and his army to Paris.

At 3:00 A.M. on January 7, 1649, for their safety's sake, Mazarin sent Anne and Louis out of the city to the dismantled palace of Saint-Germain, where they had to sleep on folding cots they had brought with them. Later they had to pawn their jewels in order to buy food and had to dismiss their servants.

Condé, who could easily have taken Paris, was restrained from doing so by Mazarin. The cardinal feared the destruction that an attack on the city would cause. Condé, therefore, only captured the fortified suburb of Charenton, thus cutting off the food supply of Paris. He then began a siege of the city.

Many nobles supported the Fronde in the hope of regain-ing from Parlement the feudal privileges that Richelieu had stripped from them. These nobles made the mistake of appeal-ing to France's recent enemies, Spain and the Holy Roman Empire, for aid against Condé.

Such disloyalty, plus a reluctance to restore rights that could lead to a repetition of the anarchy that had troubled France before Richelieu, induced Parlement to listen to the peace terms that Mazarin was offering. The two sides compromised, and a peace treaty was signed at Rueil on April 1, 1649. The king and his mother returned to the Palais-Royal on August 18, and everyone pretended that the First War of the Fronde (or the Fronde of Parlement) had been only a tiff between good friends.

The reconciliation, however, did not last long. Condé thought that his services entitled him to many rewards, among which was the right to replace Mazarin with his own protégé. Condé was a man to be reckoned with, not only because he controlled an army, but also because he was in line for the throne—after Louis, Philippe, and the aged Gaston d'Orléans. Condé's intrigues caused Mazarin to arrest and imprison him, along with his brother and his brother-in-law, the Duc de Longueville, with whom he had conspired. They were taken into custody on the morning of January 18, 1650. The Duchesse de Longueville, however, escaped Mazarin's police net and went to Normandy, where she formed an army from the peasants of her husband's estates.

On February 1, eleven-year-old King Louis XIV led his first military expedition to crush this insurrection of his cousin's. He succeeded in suppressing it within three weeks. He then went to Burgundy, where Condé's followers were in revolt against the regency. While Louis was inspecting his loyal troops who were besieging Bellegarde, a shot from the rebels on the town's walls killed an officer who was standing close beside the young king.

The Duchesse de Longueville, defeated in Normandy, proceeded to turn her charms on Henri de La Tour d'Auvergne, Vicomte de Turenne, the great military rival of Condé. A re-

markable general both in siegecraft and in field battle, Turenne
had won many victories for France during the latter part of
the Thirty Years' War. The duchess succeeded in seducing
Turenne into acquiring an army of Spaniards and putting it
into the field against Mazarin.

Condé's wife raised most of the south-central part of
France into revolt, and with her army captured the important
port of Bordeaux. The Second War of the Fronde (or the
Fronde of the Princes) had now begun in earnest. It might
have been called the Fronde of the Princesses, for women had
engineered it. Later the Grande Mademoiselle would join
them and hold her city of Orléans against the forces of the
regency.

Seeing things going against him, Mazarin released the
princes from their prison in Le Havre on February 11, 1651.
He then went into voluntary exile, stealing out of Paris by
night in the disguise of a musketeer. He took with him the
crown diamonds, and also the thirty-two-year-old Jean Baptiste
Colbert, who would later prove to be a far greater asset to
Louis XIV than the jewels. Colbert's responsibility was to
provide a liaison between the cardinal and the royalists in
Paris.

The liberated Condé returned to Paris and seized control
of the city. Fearing that the queen regent would leave the
capital to join Mazarin and would take the young king with
her, Condé's partisan, the future Cardinal de Retz, raised a
mob to prevent their departure.

Anne of Austria was indeed preparing to leave, and Louis
was in riding clothes ready to go with her, when de Retz's
mob battered at the gates of the Palais-Royal.

The queen popped her son, fully clothed, into bed and
told him to pretend to be asleep. Then she covered her

traveling clothes with a negligee and ordered the palace gates opened. She herself guided the enraged citizens into Louis's bedroom and showed them their "sleeping" king.

The sight calmed the mob. They stared at their god in silence, then left quietly and humbly, offering a prayer for the protection of the sovereign. Anne then invited two of the agitators to watch with her through the night and amused them until dawn.

Mazarin directed the government by mail from his refuge in Brühl, near Cologne. His masterstroke was to arrange for Louis XIV to declare his majority as soon as he reached the age of thirteen. Thus outmaneuvered, Condé withdrew from Paris to his estates on the Loire River, where he planned to raise a rebellion.

On September 7, 1651, Louis XIV and his entire court— except Condé—attended mass in the Sainte-Chapelle and then moved next door to the chamber where Parlement met.

Noticing Condé's absence, the queen mother exclaimed: "Either he dies or I do." She was not in the best of moods. A short while earlier, Louis had had his first love affair—with a lady of the queen's household, the Comtesse de Frontenac, whom Anne had dismissed before things went too far. Louis and his mother had had a row over her interference.

"When I am master—and that will be soon—I shall do what I want," Louis had shouted at his mother.

Anne could see her son drifting away from her. She wept. Louis wept. Then both made up the quarrel.

To his Parlement Louis said, less angrily: "I have come to tell you that in accordance with the law of my state, I am going to take the government upon myself, and I hope that with God's grace it will be managed with piety and justice." Then to the queen he said: "Madame, I thank you for the care you have been pleased to take of my education and the administration of my kingdom. I ask you to continue to give me your good counsel."

On September 13, the king led his army southward against Condé. Feeling more secure, Mazarin, who had refused a bribe to join the king of Spain's diplomatic service, raised an army and joined the court at Poitiers in January, 1652.

Desultory fighting during the winter and early spring of 1652 devastated the countryside. The common people were in greater misery than that Omer Talon had complained about in 1648. Soldiers pillaged the churches, ravished even ten-year-old peasant girls, and burned houses and barns—sometimes with the inhabitants and animals inside them. Peasants, whose crops had been bad anyway, could not harvest what survived the trampling and were reduced to eating dogs, "mud bread" made from oats they picked up from the ground, and even human corpses. Condé threw his prisoners into the icy rivers or stripped them naked to die of cold on land. All this horror the young king saw and remembered.

Condé defeated the royal army at Bléneau on May 4, 1652. Then he made the mistake of marching on Paris, which Turenne held. By that time, Turenne had gone back over to the king's side. The war now became a contest between the two rival generals of France's forces in the recently ended Thirty Years' War.

A third party was headed by the Grande Mademoiselle, who took over its leadership from her aged and ineffectual father, Gaston d'Orléans, the king's uncle. The Grande Mademoiselle seized Paris' prison-fortress, the Bastille, and turned its guns on Turenne's troops, while Condé's marched into the capital on July 2.

Once in possession of Paris, Condé overplayed his hand.

The citizens rose against him because of the destruction his mostly foreign soldiers wreaked on their city.

Peace would then have been possible if it had not been for Mazarin, whom all parties wanted out of power. Recognizing that he was a stumbling block to both the princes and the populace, Mazarin cleverly went into voluntary exile again in August.

Peace negotiations proceeded rapidly after that. On October 21, Louis and his mother reentered Paris in full state. Citizens broke through the lines of troops along the royal route to kiss the boots of their god as he rode on horseback to his palace.

Most of the rebellious nobles were pardoned. Condé, however, was exiled. The Grande Mademoiselle and her father, Gaston d'Orléans, who had fumbled his part in the rebellion, were ordered to keep to their estates. Condé, who proceeded to sell his services to the king of Spain, went on fighting on the Spanish Netherlands frontier, where he was opposed by Turenne. Otherwise, except in Guyenne, where fighting continued for several months, peace returned to the harassed kingdom of France. In early 1653, Mazarin returned to Paris to resume direction of the government and to supervise the king's education in politics.

The Second War of the Fronde utterly destroyed any hope the nobles had of regaining power and privilege. It also wiped out the few gains the Parlementaires had won toward a limited monarchy after the First War of the Fronde. The young king never forgot or truly forgave the indignities and the disloyalties he had experienced during the two rebellions. Throughout the rest of his long life he distrusted the nobles, even, and perhaps more fully, when they were his close blood relatives. Furthermore, he grew quick to suppress any idea or activity that smacked of interference with his designs. The ultimate irony of the wars of the Fronde, therefore, was that the democratic ideal for which they were fought ended in the creation of absolute royal power.

With the complete cooperation of Louis and his mother, Mazarin set to work laying strong foundations for that absolutism. His first, and perhaps most important, step was the creation of a new army. The Fronde of the Princes proved, if nothing else, that the king must never again permit his relatives or other nobles of his kingdom to be in a position where they could be more powerfully armed than he.

The crown had emerged from the rebellions victorious. It was clear, however, that it would not remain so unless the privileged of the realm—essentially the high nobility—were reduced in power. During the wars of the Fronde, the middle classes of French society—professional and business men and the small landowners—had shown that they were interested in law and order. Such, they believed, would guarantee their financial security. It appeared advisable to Mazarin, therefore, to entrust the administration of the government to members of that class. Mazarin was aiming at a strong and loyal civil service to replace old-style administrators who might be, glamorous personally but who were also self-interested.

One of the causes of the Second War of the Fronde had been the princes' objections to control by the *intendants*, the permanent agents of the crown in the provinces of France, of legal and financial matters. Mazarin shrewdly deduced that those objections were due to the inability of the nobles to share in the wealth that it was now possible to acquire through banking and trade. The aristocracy, whose wealth derived from immense landholdings, thought it beneath their dignity to engage in those pursuits. The *intendants*, however, fostered that increase in money. Consequently, Mazarin strengthened the system of *intendants*. He thus extended the power of the crown into every part of the realm, brought the royal treasury great revenue from taxes on the new money, and made the nobles virtually powerless even on their own vast estates.

The nobles were to be compensated with the privilege of being constantly in the company of the king. Too unimaginative to foresee that the honor of being kept in confinement at the king's court meant that their influence in the kingdom and their chances for personal achievement were being hourly sapped, the aristocracy gladly took this bait. Privilege, rank, and petty patronage meant everything to that decaying class. Thus began the institution of the king's court, which reached its peak in the 1680's when Louis XIV located his court permanently in Versailles. Louis wanted it away from Paris, where trouble could be fomented, and even farther away from other fortified and relatively independent cities where the nobles might find followers.

A strong army, a bureaucratic administration, the penetration of royal authority into the provinces, and the isolation of the nobility were the sides of the pyramid of absolutism that Mazarin now proceeded to build. Its stones were to be cemented by unity—one king, one law, one religion. The capstone was to be the king himself, both as a person and as an ideal.

Mazarin dedicated himself to the training of his godson— who was perhaps also his stepson—so that Louis might acquire and hold that pinnacle of power. The next eight years were the most formative of Louis XIV's life in that the pattern of his policies throughout his true reign of fifty-four years was set then.

Mazarin may have honestly loved Louis as a person, for the shrewd cardinal's affections derived from the somewhat obsequious respect he felt for anyone more elevated than he and also able. Deference to rank was as much a part of the spirit of those times as the superstitious veneration of the king as a father figure.

According to Louis's valet La Porte, the young king was once terrified of Mazarin and hated him. Now, however, he came to admire and respect his tutor in the art of government. He wrote to his friends that the cardinal was "the best friend I have in the world."

Louis was an apt pupil, worthy of the cardinal-statesman's efforts. Mazarin, who had served several potentates, said of Louis: "He has the stuff of four kings in him." He would write to Louis: "You can become the greatest king . . ." "God has given you talents . . ." "God has given you all the qualities for greatness; you must put them to use, and that you can easily do. . . . When you are at the helm of state, you will do more in one day than a cleverer person than I could do in six months." He urged Louis to fulfill his destiny, his *gloire*; his letters to the king frequently say: "You owe God and your *gloire*. . . ."

Gloire, which can be literally translated as "glory," had for the seventeenth-century man of integrity many other dimensions of meaning. It signified the completion of the individual through action and accomplishment. The ideal of the "Renaissance man" of the two previous centuries was to be proficient in many different fields. The "Baroque* man" of the seventeenth century, largely because of the religious revival of the Counter Reformation, was to be a unit, an integrated personality driving single-mindedly toward the salvation of his immortal soul, working indefatigably for a splendid reward.

---

* The word *baroque* literally signifies "irregular"; that is, varying from rigid rules of proportion and order, as a baroque pearl—from which the term originated—is not a perfect globe, but uneven in texture and bumpy in shape. In spirit, baroque represents emotionalism and excitement and activity rather than rest and tranquillity.

The seventeenth century, the age of the baroque, demanded splendor. Splendor was to the baroque mind the earthly token of the glory of Heaven. Get the one, and you could be surer of the other.

The age also put great emphasis on style, called *panache* (literally a plume for a helmet or a hat), and perhaps on insincerity. A man should be an actor, playing a part in a handsome costume. Genuine simplicity, naïveté, lack of sophistication or elegance, were considered flaws of character and behavior. Largely due to the influence of the Jesuits, the "soldiers of the Counter Reformation"—and vastly different from the Jesuits of today—variations from strict morality were condoned in a Catholic society. The end of *gloire* was everything; the means and the cost of achieving it were of secondary importance.

Mazarin's fundamental principles of education were application, attention, and hard work. He insisted that Louis love his royal duties and take pleasure in the affairs of state. His method was to make the king an active participant in these. He saw to it that Louis was present at council meetings, read dispatches and studied documents, considered alternatives, learned to use his own judgment, and reasoned things out by himself.

Louis and Mazarin were together almost uninterruptedly during those eight years. After the king rose and had his daily exercise on horseback and with weapons, they met in Mazarin's apartments just above Louis's in the Palais-Royal. In those conferences they discussed problems of state. Thus Louis learned from the wide and deep experience of the older diplomat how to estimate another ruler's character and motives and predict his actions—to be able to tell which way the cat would jump. He also picked up from the cardinal many minor points of successful ruling, such as the necessity of being always polite and considerate, answering all communications promptly, keeping a pocket notebook in which to jot ideas, never giving an immediate direct answer. Hence, Louis XIV's most characteristic reply to any request, "*Je verrai*" (I will see).

On his deathbed, Mazarin dictated rules for the good of the state that he hoped the king whom he had so devotedly coached would follow: Pick worthy men for all offices and continually check on their private and public behavior; keep the nobility a useful tool; hold the judges in line; reward faithful servitors; care for the taxpayers' persons and interests as a means of controlling them, but without emotional involvement.

Mazarin also counseled Louis never to have a prime minister. Probably this ironic advice was due to Mazarin's pride in having developed a king who, he believed, could rule by himself. It was doubtless also due to the cardinal's vanity; he did not wish to be succeeded by a prime minister who might surpass himself.

In spite of this manifestation of pride, and the pride he took in the magnificent collection of works of art he assembled, Mazarin, the son of a household servant, always kept the ideal of service and humility. "God," he insisted to Louis, "did not establish kings so that they could gratify their own desires, but as His servants."

Louis, in turn, would instruct his own son: "You cannot show too much respect for Him who has made us respected. . . . The first lesson in politics teaches us to serve Him well. . . . God has His own *gloire*, and is very jealous of it."

III

A KING'S LOVE
AND A KING'S MARRIAGE

With Condé and his Spanish army harassing the northern frontier of France, Mazarin saw the political advantage of checking the spread of allegiance to that prince of the blood by a grand public ceremony that would revive loyalty to King Louis XIV. Such ceremonies had worked well in the past to arouse the emotions of the French. Consequently the cardinal set the coronation of the king for June 7, 1654.

The great cathedral of Rheims had been the traditional spot for the coronation of French kings since Clovis, the founder of the monarchy, was anointed there in 496 by Saint Rémy with oil supposedly brought from heaven by a dove. The court, including the foreign ambassadors, moved to Rheims for the occasion several days before the event itself.

That began at 4:40 A.M., with the richly robed clergy reciting the first offices of the day. By 6:00 A.M., the cathedral was jammed with invited spectators. The bishops then led a procession to the palace where Louis was housed, demanding "the king, Louis XIV, son of the great king, Louis XIII, whom God has given us for king." After three repetitions of that formal request, they were admitted to Louis's bedroom, where they found him already magnificently attired in white. The bishops and clergy, chanting, praying, and scattering holy water, then led Louis to the church amid the smoke of incense and the sound of flutes, oboes, and drums.

Gorgeous tapestries, still to be seen in the museum of Rheims, screened the high altar from the masses of people in the nave who could see the pageant only through the small "door" by which the procession entered the choir of the cathedral. A high balcony had been erected within that section, where sat the official guests. In a box were the queen mother and the deposed queen of England, Henrietta Maria, widow of Charles I and Louis's aunt.

The throne, just in front of the high altar, was set on a platform covered with rich oriental rugs. Upon it streamed the summer sunlight, infinitely tinted by the famous stained glass of the beautiful rose window above. On either side were benches on which sat the clergy, the peers of France, the generals, and the high officials of the royal government.

Louis prostrated himself before the altar, as if he were a priest being ordained, while three generals held the crown, the sword, and the scepter of France. The trumpets blared, and the drums thundered. Then, after the *Agnus Dei* of the mass, the grand prior of the Abbey of Saint-Rémy offered the king the vial of holy oil.

Louis was then covered with the gold-embroidered velvet robe of office, given the symbols of sovereignty, and placed on the throne to receive the reverence of the cardinals and dukes— the kiss of peace, wine, "bread" of silver and gold, and a purse of thirteen gold coins. Singing birds were released to soar into the lofty vaults of the cathedral, and showers of money were tossed to the people.

The anointment of a king signified, as it had since the ancient times of the Hebrews, that he was thus endowed with the gifts and graces of the Spirit, chosen by God to be His representative—a truly holy being, whose person was sacred and whose words and will expressed God's purposes. Louis was never to allow anyone to forget the sacred significance of the coronation ceremony.

Two months later, Louis went to the battlefront to watch Turenne relieve Arras, which Condé was besieging. Louis was no bold and courageous military leader, as his grandfather and his father had been and as, ironically, his effeminate brother was to be. He was merely a spectator, sometimes in the way, always something of an embarrassment to the generals and colonels who had to put his physical safety ahead of their own military operations. But Louis let Turenne, one of the ablest generals of history, teach him much about warfare, and he took pride and pleasure in managing his armies—on paper.

Louis was considerably more resolute in his early approaches to Parlement. In April, 1655, he held, on his own initiative, a *lit de justice* to suppress a Fronde-like attitude to the taxes he requested. He was so forceful that Mazarin had to bribe the chief magistrates to prevent their starting another civil war.

While Mazarin was trying desperately to close the division in the kingdom which Condé, supported by Spain, was causing, and to leave a solidly united nation to his protégé, Louis himself almost upset the royal applecart again.

Mazarin had five nieces, the daughters of his sister Girolama, who had married an Italian nobleman, Michele Lorenzo Mancini. When Mancini died, Mazarin brought the family, his only close relatives, to the French court. Then he went to considerable pains to marry off the girls well. By 1651, he had succeeded in getting a husband for the eldest, Laure—none other than an illegitimate grandson of Henry IV and therefore a cousin of Louis XIV. She became the mother of Louis's brilliant general the Duc de Vendome during the latter years of his reign.

This marriage notwithstanding, Louis was very attracted to Laure—so much so that, at a court ball in 1655, Anne of Austria had to forbid her seventeen-year-old son to dance with Laure any longer. The queen mother insisted that, out of politeness at least, he also dance with his English cousin Henriette, who was then eleven years old. Louis protested that Henriette was only a skinny little girl. That opinion he later revised; in fact, he fell quite in love with her after Henriette married his brother Philippe.

Louis then turned his attentions to Laure's eighteen-year-old sister Olympe. Olympe Mancini, however, turned the tables on Louis by snubbing him as too young for her. She also had no intention of spoiling her chances of marrying the royal-blooded Prince of Savoy and Count of Soissons. By him she became the mother of the distinguished general, Prince Eugene of Savoy, who fought against France in the War of the Spanish Succession.

Louis next had a fling with Mlle de La Motte, a none too chaste blue-eyed blonde—clearly a rebound from the dark Mancini girls. Mazarin promptly stuck her into a convent. Louis then discovered Marie, the Cinderella of the Mancini family, the third in age of Mazarin's nieces.

Anne of Austria's close companion, Mme de Motteville, wrote of Marie Mancini about 1656 that the sixteen-year-old girl was extremely thin, had a long neck and long arms, a sallow complexion, big black eyes that lacked expression, and a large shapeless mouth. To Louis, however, Marie Mancini had compensating merits. She kindled his imagination by reading novels and plays to him. She even made him ashamed of his ignorance of literature. Her lively wit so amused him that he could not bear the boredom of being out of her company for more than a day. Through Marie he found that his previously poor opinion of women in general was mistaken. Marie would not yield to his propositions.

In the summer of 1658, Louis became seriously ill from a fever he got from the vile sanitary conditions of the camp while he was watching the siege of Dunkirk, which Turenne won from Condé. When Louis learned that Marie had wept over his close brush with death and had prayed for his recovery, amusement and admiration changed into love. The two adolescents became inseparable.

Louis's illness terrified Mazarin and Anne of Austria. What if he had died, leaving no heir but his effeminate brother, who would be quickly dethroned by Condé? They determined that Louis must rapidly take a royal bride and beget an heir to the throne.

Mazarin had his eyes on Maria Theresa, daughter of King Philip IV of Spain and Anne of Austria's niece. Such a union would presumably end the eternal warfare between Spain and France and join the rival dynasties of Hapsburg and Bourbon. But Mazarin was too wily to rush into the masterstroke of diplomacy. And he was far too practical a politician to be diverted by so sentimental a consideration as Louis's noticeable affection for Marie Mancini. Marie would bring to the potentially great king whom Mazarin had created nothing but love.

Philip IV was as eager as his sister Anne and Cardinal Mazarin for a marriage between Louis and Maria Theresa, but he would not make peace, which was Mazarin's condition for the union. Philip was under pressure from the Dutch, who did not want France in control of the adjacent Spanish Netherlands. Turenne's continued military successes in that region indicated that the French might soon be unwelcome neighbors to the Dutch.

Consequently Mazarin invented an engagement between

Louis and another of the king's cousins, Princess Marguerite of Savoy. In the fall of 1658, the cardinal arranged an elaborate "house party" at Lyons for the two families. He particularly wanted the two young people to meet and, he hoped, fall into each other's arms. Mazarin took pains to see that Philip IV heard all about this family gathering.

At first, Louis was rather taken with Princess Marguerite, and he paid her much more attention than he ordinarily gave to other women. Marie Mancini's clever rejoinder to that situation was: "Aren't you ashamed to be forced into marriage with such an ugly girl?" Marie herself, according to portraits of her, had changed from Mme de Motteville's earlier description of her into a beauty.

Louis agreed. The two lovers became as inseparable as before and spent most of their time riding horseback in the October-tinted forests around Lyons.

Just as Mazarin had hoped, Philip IV fell into the trap the cardinal had set for him. As soon as the Spanish monarch heard of the house party, he dispatched a courier at top speed to Lyons with the message that a peace treaty was now not unlikely and that he favored the marriage of his daughter to the French king.

Informed that the peace of Europe was more important than a marriage to the royal family of Savoy, that contingent left Lyons with rather poor grace. Their disgruntlement is understandable in view of the fact that Anne of Austria had decided earlier that Princess Marguerite was not good enough for her son and so had been quite cool to her sister-in-law, the princess's mother. When the French court returned to Paris, Louis and Marie Mancini were in a carriage by themselves.

Louis and Marie continued in their mutual infatuation,

which led them to the fond hope that the Spanish marriage would never take place and that Mazarin would somehow permit his star pupil to marry his niece. Such a match, the lovesick Louis reasoned, would be no more than what was due the cardinal for all he had done for the Bourbon family.

It finally dawned on Anne and Mazarin that Louis was completely serious about Marie. The cardinal quickly proposed to pack Marie off to Brouages, far to the southwest of Paris, and to send Louis to the Condé palace at Chantilly, twenty-five miles northeast of the capital. Anne broke the plan to Louis in the privacy of her bathroom. After an hour of tearful pleading she won his grudging consent to the separation.

The lovers parted on June 22, 1659. The king escorted Marie Mancini to her carriage. For a long time he leaned on its window, weeping.

"Ah, Sire," Marie said proudly, "you may weep, but I must go."

As the carriage started up, Marie tore the lace cuff from Louis's sleeve and burst out, "I have been deserted."

The divided lovers corresponded frequently and passionately. More than one of Louis's young friends was sent away from court for having counseled the king to elope with Marie and free himself from the cardinal. Even Queen Christina of Sweden, who was visiting the French court then, urged Louis to follow his heart and marry the girl.

Spies, among whom was Marie's younger sister Hortense, carried the gist of the lovers' letters to Mazarin. Even worse, they kept the king of Spain informed. Philip IV threatened to repudiate his offers of peace and marriage.

Mazarin, therefore, was forced to play his trump card— threaten to resign. Louis pleaded for one last meeting with Marie. While Mazarin was in Spain negotiating the peace treaty, Anne consented to that reunion—much to the cardinal's horror, for he was worldy wise enough to foresee that such a rendezvous would be more likely to rekindle the lovers' devotion to each other rather than quench it. He was right; the meeting in early August only made Louis more determined than ever to defy the cardinal.

Mazarin now wrote more forcibly than ever to Louis, protesting that a marriage with Marie would so damage the king's *gloire*, not to mention his kingdom, that it would be an affront to God and would bring down His wrath upon France.

On September 3, Marie herself decided that the Spanish marriage was as good as accomplished. If Louis would not face reality, it was up to her to do so. She sent word to Louis that she would write to him no more and begged him not to write to her. Louis, at first, did not believe her and sent her his little dog to prove his devotion. But Marie was firm. Each burned the other's letters.

The cardinal's joy over the broken romance was dimmed by his fear that Louis's despair would make him refuse the Infanta Maria Theresa. But Anne of Austria proved to be right when she had said after the bathroom interview: "I pity the king. He is both loving and reasonable, and God gave him the loftiness necessary for him to be a great king." Louis XIV resigned himself to his patriotic duty. His flagrant extramarital affairs during the next twenty years, however, seem to have been his desperate attempt to get rid of the bitter taste of the pill he had had to swallow in giving up the one true love of his life.

In January, 1660, Mazarin negotiated a marriage between Marie Mancini and Prince Lorenzo Colonna, constable of Naples, of the same family that had once employed the young

Giulio Mazarini and his father. Louis and Marie had been allowed to meet again, but court gossips were instructed to inform each of them that the other was quite happy with the new arrangements.

As Marie prepared to ride off to Italy with her new husband, Louis XIV did her the honor of seeing her to her carriage. He said not a word to her, only heaved a deep sigh, and bowed deeply as he handed her into the vehicle. Marie, however, burst into tears. She deserted her husband in 1672, but Louis refused to receive her at his court. She died in Italy in 1715.

The terms of the treaty of peace between France and Spain having been concluded, only the marriage of Louis XIV and the Infanta Maria Theresa of Spain stood in the way of its being signed. In the negotiations Spain had demanded the restoration of the exiled Prince de Condé to his titles, honors, wealth, and lands in France. Louis, who regarded Condé as a traitor, made Spain pay dearly for this condition with many fortified towns in the Spanish Netherlands. Condé returned, fully pardoned, on January 27, 1660.

Spain was also to pay France, as a dowry for Maria Theresa, the then staggering sum of 500,000 écus (approximately $4,000,000 at today's values and purchasing power). In return for this dowry, the infanta was to renounce her claim to the Spanish throne, for the laws of Spain, unlike those of France, permitted a woman to wear the crown.

All in all, the treaty was Mazarin's masterpiece of diplomacy. The House of Hapsburg was not to be subordinated to the House of Bourbon, as Richelieu would have demanded, but allied with it, even though the Bourbons were the major partner. This arrangement consolidated the Catholic and Mediterranean countries of Europe and also allowed France to keep its alliance with Protestant England. As king of France, Louis XIV would be the arbiter of a finally pacified Europe.*

Louis was, therefore, eager to get on with a marriage which would assure that position for him. Months of preparation for the wedding, however, were necessary to suit the strict protocol and rigid etiquette of the Spanish court. It was not until late in the spring of 1660 that the royal family of France and the French court set out toward the Pyrenees. The tour—a fine piece of propaganda—gave Louis his first glimpse of the south of France and the Mediterranean with its trading cities and the great French fleet of merchant galleys.**

The treaty was to be signed on June 6, 1660, on the Isle of Pheasants in the Bidassoa River, through which ran the boundary line between France and Spain. Neither king could

---

* Politically, Europe then consisted of the Protestant nations: England, the United Provinces (later called Holland), Denmark, Sweden (including Norway and Finland), and about half of the 300-odd independent principalities to which were given the geographical name of Germany. The Catholic countries were France; Spain, including the Spanish Netherlands (Belgium); Italy south of Rome (the kingdom of Naples and Sicily); and Austria, the Catholic part of the Holy Roman Empire and northern Italy. The Empire had disintegrated after the Peace of Westphalia in 1648, though the ruler of Austria kept the title of emperor and his realm was still called the Empire. Eastern Europe (Russia, Hungary, Poland) was not involved in general European politics until later in the seventeenth century. Most of the Balkan Peninsula was in the hands of the Muslim Turks, as were the eastern Mediterranean islands, including Crete and Cyprus. Minor Catholic political entities were the Papal States of central Italy, and Savoy (a principality bounded, roughly, by Nice on the west, Geneva on the north, and Pavia on the east). Protestant Switzerland was neutral.

** These armed ships, the fastest afloat until the coming of steam-powered vessels, had a shallow draft which made them ideal landing craft. Since they did not depend upon wind for locomotion, they were highly maneuverable, good for attack, patrol, and removing damaged battleships from a naval engagement. They were propelled chiefly by oars manned mostly by convicts who were often maltreated but generally fared better than is usually believed—if they survived the strain of rowing, the foul conditions aboard ship, and the whip of the officers.

leave his kingdom by so much as an inch, even for so important an occasion, and so the table for the signing was set over the exact line. For the meeting between the Spanish king and the French queen mother, two rugs were laid on either side of the line, and brother and sister leaned across the slight gap to kiss each other after having been separated for forty-five years.

Since protocol forbade a Spanish princess to leave her country until she was married, a marriage by proxy had been celebrated at Fuentarrabia, Spain, on June 2, 1660. Then, on June 7, after the treaty had been signed, the bride was handed over to her new family. Previously, Louis and Maria Theresa had seen each other only for a moment, and then by a ruse arranged by Louis's brother Philippe, who had inherited the title of Duc d'Orléans upon the death of his uncle Gaston on February 2, 1660, and who was now known as "Monsieur."

Flattery was so essential in all relationships with the twenty-one-year-old king of France—and for the rest of his life—that it is hard today to get a true picture of him either from the artists who painted his portrait or the writers who described him. One visitor was so impressed by Louis's regal manner that he recorded the king's height as six feet. Louis's armor, however, demonstrates that he was actually five feet five inches tall at the time of his marriage and later shrank with age to five feet four.

A composite of all the pen and paint portraits of Louis XIV indicates that in 1660 he had broad shoulders, a full chest, well-proportioned and robust arms and legs. His eyes were dark and piercing. In spite of smallpox scars, his complexion was good, his beard was still downy, his light-brown long hair thick and wavy.

Louis's expression was said to be "sweet and majestic," his manner cold and reserved. He talked little except to his

Louis XIV at the time of his marriage, 1660.

intimates; he chose his words well, stuck to his subject, and was an excellent raconteur. He was infallibly polite, considerate, and generous. It appears that he was also a little diffident.

Maria Theresa is best known to the world from Velásquez's famous portrait of her, of which several versions exist. In the enormous wig and the even more enormous dress built on a

Maria Theresa of Spain (1638–83), first wife of Louis XIV, by Velásquez. Louvre, Paris.

wide wire framework that were the Spanish fashion, she looks like a costume doll. She had little more intelligence than one, and what brains she did possess were so untrained that she appeared a simpleton. She was small, but she had a good figure, a white skin, blue eyes, and a rather large but pretty mouth. Utterly lacking in wit or any other social charm, and unable to speak French (Louis could barely speak Spanish), her only merit as a wife to the dashing Louis was the fact that she was head over heels in love with him.

The French court escorted the royal pair to Saint-Jean-de-Luz, on French soil, where they were married in a fairy-tale ceremony on June 9. The path from the palace to the church was covered with oriental rugs and lined with white-and-gold poles draped with garlands. The Prince de Conti, Condé's younger brother, led the procession, followed by Cardinal Mazarin in scarlet and an ermine cloak. Then followed, at a distance, King Louis XIV, dressed in cloth of gold covered with black net, walking soberly and majestically. After him came Maria Theresa, between the Duc d'Orléans and the head of her household. Her dress was of silver brocade, over which she wore a cloak of purple velvet embroidered with gold fleur-de-lys. Its twenty-foot-long train was carried by two duchesses and one princess. Two other duchesses held the crown above her blonde hair.

Behind the bride walked Louis's mother and Maria Theresa's aunt, Anne of Austria, in black embroidered with silver. Last came the Grande Mademoiselle, her mourning, which she wore for her late father, enlivened by twenty ropes of pearls.

After the ceremony, performed by the bishop of Bayonne, there was a great royal banquet, during which the king and his queen frequently stepped to a balcony to throw money to the cheering crowds. The feast was not over when Louis whispered to his bride that it was time for bed.

"Too early," she replied, a little shocked. But she left immediately for her room, where she told her maids to undress her quickly. "Hurry, hurry," she kept saying, "the king is waiting."

Louis XIV always treated his queen with kindness and

respect and visited her regularly at least twice a month. Love her, however, he did not. She was no replacement for the lost Marie Mancini. In fact, when the bridal entourage stopped near Brouages, Louis went there to spend the night of June 28 in the house where his beloved had stayed. Until late, he walked the beach, sobbing as if his heart would break, then crawled into the bed Marie once had warmed.

The return of the king to Paris with his bride was the occasion for another grand celebration which took place on August 26, 1660. The French now had not only peace but a queen. Outside the city walls that morning, Louis received the homage of the representatives of Paris, the clergy, the professors of the university, the guilds, the judges, the mint, the tax department, and Parlement. Their spokesmen delivered flowery orations of praise and welcome. Then those bodies, all in their robes of office, and the priests chanting, led a procession to escort the king and queen into the city itself.

Behind them came the gentlemen and guards of Cardinal Mazarin's household, riding seventy-two gorgeously caparisoned mules in twenty-four rows. The queen mother's household and animals followed. After her rode the king's household and the members of his government on sixty mules and twenty-four horses. Among them was Chancellor Pierre Séguier, shaded with golden parasols carried by six youths who marched beside his gold-covered horse. Then came soldiers, courtiers, governors of provinces, the Hundred Swiss of the royal bodyguard, and the generals.

The king himself rode on horseback, followed by the Duc d'Orléans, the Prince de Conti, the Duc d'Enghien, and the renegade Prince de Condé—all with their officers. Behind them a chariot drawn by six gray horses carried the queen in a golden robe covered with pearls and jewels. After her were carriages containing the ladies of rank in France, the foreign princesses, and the wives of the peers of the realm. The procession ended with more soldiers and the king's huntsmen. It took four hours for the parade to pass a given point.

Along the route of the procession were gorgeous triumphal arches decorated with allegorical groups and topped with bands of musicians. One arch was sixty by forty-eight feet; another, painted to resemble white marble, was surmounted with an obelisk. The whole pageant was the wonder of the age—the age of the baroque, which it so completely typified. No one who saw it ever forgot it or that it symbolized peace and a God-anointed king and his bride.

Cardinal Jules Mazarin, too worn out from his labors over the events that the procession was celebrating, could not take part in it. Instead, he watched it from a balcony. Everyone knew that the fifty-nine-year-old master statesman was dying. Yet he continued to direct the difficult diplomacy necessitated by the restoration of the Stuart king to the throne of England, and to find an end for the war in Poland.

Louis and Anne of Austria moved to Vincennes, then about four miles east of Paris but now a part of the city, in order to be with the cardinal during his final illness. At 2:30 A.M. on March 9, 1661, he died, regretting only that he had to leave behind his beautiful paintings. Louis XIV ordered full state mourning for Cardinal Jules Mazarin—the only man outside the royal family ever to be so honored up to that time.

IV

THE SUN RISES

Louis XIV received word of Cardinal Mazarin's death as soon as he awoke on the morning of March 9, 1661. It is said he dressed himself without the aid of his valet and then locked himself in his study for two hours. Possibly his purpose was to get control over his emotions, for he was genuinely grieved by the passing of his mentor and friend. More likely he wanted to be alone in order to plan his immediate measures in obedience to the late cardinal's oft-repeated advice that the duty of a king is to act.

Now that Louis was the sole ruler of France, determined—also in obedience to Mazarin's counsel—to act alone, he doubtless remembered again his disgust at the ancient French rulers, known as the "do-nothing" kings, whose stories La Porte had read to him from Mézeray's history. When he emerged from his period of uncustomary solitude, he sent word to the secretaries of state, the minister of finance, the chancellor, and the foreign minister, requesting their presence at a meeting with him in the Louvre in Paris at seven o'clock on the following morning.

Much later, Louis confessed that he was terrified by the

very thought of addressing those old and experienced government officials, and that it took him a long time to grow used to speaking authoritatively to them and in public. Mazarin had hitherto always done that for him. Something of Louis's timidity appears in the formal and precise phrases he used, but no one could doubt the firmness of his intentions and his directives to his administrators.

"I have called you together," Louis said, standing to open the meeting, "to tell you that up to the present it has pleased me to entrust the government *of my affairs* to the late cardinal. *It is now time that I govern them myself.* You will assist me with your counsels *when I ask for them.* . . . I order you not to sign anything . . . without my command, *to report to me personally every day,* and to favor no one [emphasis supplied]."

The italicized passages in this speech might have been condensed into the famous phrase so often attributed to Louis XIV, but probably never uttered by him: "*L'état, c'est moi*" (I am the state). Louis's first address as master of his kingdom present and future was a masterful way of declaring that his mastery was not to be challenged. For the first time in nearly fifty years France had a truly governing king.

Louis confirmed this supremacy later in the same conference by his reply to the president of the assembly of the clergy, who had asked to whom he should go for decisions: "To me. To me."

Without a prime minister to assemble a cabinet for him, Louis, who knew but had not yet announced that there was to be no such officer, had to create an administrative organization by himself. Perhaps in his two hours of communing with himself, he decided to use the men whom Mazarin had appointed and trained.

The most important of those was Nicolas Fouquet, the *surintendant des finances* or, as an American would have called

Nicolas Fouquet (1615–80).

him, secretary of the treasury. Forty-six years old in 1661, Fouquet, who was of the newer nobility (*noblesse de la robe*), had won Mazarin's patronage by his loyalty to the cardinal during the upheavals of the Fronde. He had held his office since 1653.

Fouquet was a supremely ambitious man, whose emblem was a squirrel and whose motto was *quo non ascendam* ("to what heights shall I not climb?"). Intelligent and highly skilled, Fouquet had gathered around him a small army of his "creatures"—men whom he had trained and who were loyal to him first of all. This machinery, Fouquet fondly hoped, would be his means of taking over Mazarin's position after the cardinal resigned to become pope—as Mazarin had seriously planned—or died. In addition, Fouquet had acquired, through loans to them, a set of courtiers who supplied him with information.

Fouquet had imitated Mazarin by patronizing artists and writers, and by collecting art treasures. In 1657, he had gone further than the cardinal by beginning the construction of a splendid palace at Vaux-le-Vicomte, near Melun, about twenty miles southeast of Paris. He had also fortified his castle at Belle-Isle and much of the adjacent seacoast in Brittany.

Although Mazarin and Fouquet had connived in dubious manipulations of the royal money, Mazarin had probably cautioned Louis about the clever but none too wise finance minister. Probably to keep Fouquet in line, Mazarin had also favored Jean Baptiste Colbert, to whom he had given an office in the treasury next in authority to Fouquet's. Mazarin had also recommended Colbert to Louis, calling that forty-two-year-old financial wizard his most valuable legacy to the young king. In his speech to his councillors on March 10, Louis XIV specifically announced that he intended to keep Colbert in office.

Vastly different from Fouquet, Colbert was the son of a linen merchant of Rheims and typical in character and personality of the businessman class of France. Mme de Sévigné, the witty and perceptive chronicler of the Age of Louis XIV, nicknamed Colbert "Mister North Pole," so chilly was his manner and so ice hard his will.

Colbert's single goal was to secure his own position, for he had no private resources and no other means of gratifying his need to be important. A crafty schemer, he moved relentlessly toward achieving his ambition.

Louis also retained Mazarin's war minister, Michel Le Tellier, whom the cardinal used to refer to in his private correspondence as "the faithful one." Le Tellier's family were lawyers and minor government officials. He was the oldest of Louis's panel of councillors, being fifty-eight in 1661. Because of his age, Le Tellier had been assisted for the previous eight years by his son François, who would be created a marquis and thereafter be known, from the name of his estate, as Louvois.*

Father and son, therefore, made, as it were, one war minister. They were different, however. Le Tellier was soft and compromising; Louvois was as hard and as absolute in his decisions as Louis XIV himself. Louvois is often credited with much that his father accomplished, such as the bringing of discipline, systematic recruitment, and organization into the

---

* A Frenchman was often rewarded for his service to the state (i.e., the king) with the gift of a piece of land, frequently with buildings on it, which carried with it a title, generally "Marquis" (or "Marquise" if the recipient was a woman). The title belonged to the land and was transferred to a new owner with the property itself. Such persons constituted the lesser nobility. They were despised as newcomers by those who had acquired their land and title by inheritance (the *noblesse de la robe*) and by those of ancient noble lineage or of royal blood (the *noblesse de l'epée*). These distinctions of rank, which may seem ridiculous today, and the privileges that went with them, were taken with the utmost seriousness in seventeenth-century French society, and they had much to do with the influence and power of an individual.

French army. Le Tellier was a good manager and a fine strategist.

Louis's other major councillor was Hugues de Lionne, a man of the minor nobility, but so poor that he had to depend for a livelihood on royal generosity. He was, therefore, much to the king's taste. Fifty years old, Lionne had had a long, successful career in diplomacy, and he was very familiar with affairs in England, the United Provinces (Holland), Italy, and Spain. Not ambitious, he knew how to please the king, whom he greatly admired, and also how to keep things from Louis when he knew he could handle them better himself. As foreign minister, Lionne had considerable influence on Louis XIV.

This group of advisers and administrators contained no member of the clergy. Again, Louis was following Mazarin's advice in excluding the Church. Neither wanted a man in a position of power whose allegiance was primarily to the pope, who might be friendly or hostile to France's policies.

The church in France was the Gallican (i.e., French) rather than the Roman Catholic. It took spiritual direction from the pope, but the king decided its policies. The French king was known as "His Most Christian Majesty" rather than as "His Catholic Majesty," as, say, King Philip II of Spain had been in the previous century. With the loss of that great ally, the papacy had declined in political influence anyway, and the pontiffs who reigned contemporaneously with Louis XIV were more or less content to keep what influence they might in France rather than risk losing all control over affairs in that country by antagonizing Louis XIV.

Louis listened to, and was sometimes swayed by, the great French churchmen of his time, notably Bossuet and François Fénelon. Their influence, however, was almost entirely on his personal and private life rather than on his public policies.

The council of state, composed of Fouquet, Colbert, Le

Tellier (and sometimes Louvois), and Lionne, met at least three times a week and sometimes four—in times of crisis, it met more often—to decide major matters of policy and how to activate them. Louis listened carefully to the advice of his ministers, which was based on the reports to them from minor councils, but the final decision was his, and he permitted no discussion of it.

That centralization of authority placed a heavy burden of work on the man upon whom it pivoted. Louis was not only equal to the effort, but enjoyed it. In order to have the eight or nine hours per day that he needed for state business, he established for himself a schedule from which he rarely departed. The Duc de Saint-Simon, whose memoirs furnish a minutely detailed (but sometimes inaccurate) history of Louis XIV's reign, said that one could set one's watch by the king's movements, or by looking at the same watch tell exactly what the king would be doing at that moment.

Louis's day—that is, a composite picture of it; details varied, especially as Louis XIV grew older—began at 8:00 A.M., when his valet, who slept in the king's bedroom, whispered in his ear that it was time. Then the valet advised the crowd of courtiers in the anteroom that their sovereign was awake. Two doctors then entered the bedroom to examine the king and to rub him down with rose water. (In his later years, Louis XIV sweated profusely under the piles of coverlets prescribed for his gout.) With the doctors came Louis's old nurse Pierrette Dufour, now Mme Hemelin and one of Anne of Austria's ladies-in-waiting, who would kiss him and ask him how he had slept. His answer, which was quickly broadcast, indicated what his mood for that day was likely to be. Next, the wigmaker gave Louis the short wig he would wear while he was dressing.

At eight fifteen, courtiers who were favored with the

privilege were admitted to the royal bedroom. This was the best time for any of them who wanted anything—and they all did—to bend over the king's bed and request a favor. Louis would reply, "I will see," but he rarely forgot to attend to the matter, trivial though it might be. Then Louis dismissed the courtiers while he said his prayers, after which devotions he called all the waiting courtiers into the room to watch him dress.

The king dressed himself, then washed his face and hands in scented alcohol, and shaved if it was an "odd" day. The talk among the group was generally about hunting. Once Louis's toilet was complete, everyone joined in prayers.

Louis then went into his study, where, in the space of ten minutes, he announced his activities for the day so that everyone might know where he could be found. He then dismissed all but his intimates, with whom he talked casually about the affairs of his household.

The king next proceeded to high mass in the chapel, where he usually sat in the gallery. Anyone could speak to him as he passed through the palace rooms and corridors. Immediately after mass he met with his council, or held interviews if the council was not convened, until dinnertime, generally around 1:00 P.M. He ate alone in his room, but courtiers stood about and watched him, even though he rarely spoke to any of them. The meal, which Louis ate with his fingers, was enormous.

After dinner, the king went again to his study, pausing at its door to listen to requests for interviews and perhaps granting one then and there. He would feed his dogs to be sure that they recognized him, then change his clothes for his daily exercise—stag-hunting three times a week, weather permitting; shooting; or walking in his gardens (when he grew old, he rode in a kind of wheelchair), for he loved fresh air.

When he returned indoors, he changed his clothes again,

and spent the time until supper—usually at 10:00 P.M.—in his study over correspondence.

Supper was an even more enormous meal than dinner; at one time Louis consumed four different plates of stew, a whole pheasant, a whole partridge, two slices of ham, salad, some mutton, pastry, fruit, and hard-boiled eggs (a greater delicacy then than now). The portions, however, were small; neither a pheasant nor a partridge, for example, has more than four good mouthfuls of meat on it. Louis drank very little wine and usually mixed it with water. In the morning he would have a glass of hippocras (a spiced white wine) or a cup of herb tea; and a cold buffet would be put in his room in case he felt hungry during the night; but he never ate between his two meals of the day. An autopsy revealed that his stomach was far larger than average.

After supper, Louis received in his study the persons he wished to see, then spent about an hour with his family, unless there was a court entertainment, as there usually was three times a week.

Returning to his bedroom, Louis signaled when he wished to retire by giving his famous bow to the ever-present courtiers. He nodded to the one who was to have the great privilege of holding the royal candelstick while the king undressed. Again it was a favorable time for a request to be made of the king. The royal day ended about 1:30 A.M., with everyone except Louis himself exhausted, for very, very few had the privilege of sitting in the sovereign's ubiquitous presence.

Louis XIV's first efforts in administration were devoted to straightening out the finances of the kingdom, which was then some 60,000,000 livres ($150,000,000) in debt at a time when there was no such thing as a "national debt." This obligation required 9,000,000 livres of interest to be subtracted from an annual revenue of 31,000,000 livres. For two months

Fouquet's palace of Vaux-le-Vicomte.

Louis studied the situation with Fouquet, but he was much better guided by Colbert. Colbert showed the king actual figures, whereas Fouquet was casual about details. By the beginning of May, 1661, Louis had made up his mind that Fouquet must go as soon as his dismissal could be conveniently arranged.

At Louis's request, Colbert examined Fouquet's accounts and informed the king that Fouquet had been diverting state funds into his own pocket. When Louis asked Fouquet about this practice, the finance minister replied that he was only following Mazarin's orders. Louis was obliged to accept that explanation because he had insisted that Mazarin's instructions be closely followed. One of those was that the king keep

Fouquet—and Colbert—in his service. Dipping into the public till was a common practice among treasury officials anyway.

The king thus found that he was being dominated by one of his ministers. Another confirmation of that unwelcome situation was Louis's discovery that Fouquet had attempted to bribe one of the king's intimates. Fouquet's intention was clearly to increase his power by adding a valuable informant to his already sizable list of dependents.

Fouquet thus appeared to Louis as far too powerful and unscrupulous a man to be a confidential minister. The king, remembering the Fronde, did not like the fact that Fouquet owned a fortified castle quite able to withstand an assault by the royal army. However, Louis did not dare dismiss Fouquet until he could reorganize the system of collecting taxes, which only Fouquet understood and could manage. Louis was forced to acknowledge that he would have to proceed slowly and cautiously against the potential menace of his minister.

The king's first step was to persuade Fouquet to resign his seat in Parlement, which entitled him to be tried only by his fellow judges whom he could easily corrupt if necessary. Louis did not wish any case he might be able to build against Fouquet to be heard by a court that had once started a rebellion over matters of finance and might well do so again.

Fouquet's informants undoubtedly let him know which way the royal wind was blowing. For although Louis insisted on absolute secrecy about political matters, and never discussed them with even his immediate family, the king, as the record of his usual day shows, was almost never alone, or unobserved by hundreds of people. Probably to repair his shaky relationship with the king, Fouquet gave a kind of housewarming for his palace at Vaux-le-Vicomte by which he could entertain his royal master.

To this fete, on August 17, 1661, Fouquet invited six

thousand people to meet the king. For their entertainment he provided a performance of a new play by Molière, the king's favorite dramatist; music especially written for the occasion by Lully, the king's favorite composer; food prepared by Vatel, the greatest chef in France (who later committed suicide rather than serve a dinner without the proper fish); fireworks, illuminated fountains, and gold plates for the guests. The party cost Fouquet 120,000 livres ($300,000) in a time when a family of ten could live well on 600 livres ($1,500) a year.

Entertained Louis XIV undoubtedly was, but he was very unfavorably impressed by the lavishness of the party, not to mention Fouquet's elegant palace, with its large library, its paintings and tapestries, and, above all, its elaborate gardens filled with statuary. The whole affair seemed a challenge to the king, whose own palaces were shabby in contrast. Louis XIV did not enjoy being challenged by his nobles, even so minor a member of the nobility as Nicolas Fouquet.

Louis would have had Fouquet arrested on the spot if his mother had not restrained him. Perhaps Anne of Austria reminded her son that he had only circumstantial evidence of the finance minister's peculations.

In less than a month, however, Louis had all the concrete evidence against Fouquet that he thought he needed. He decided to strike against the minister on the very ground where Fouquet thought himself most safe. Louis summoned his council to meet on September 5 at Nantes, near Fouquet's fortified domain, and had him arrested there by Charles de Baatz, Sieur d'Artagnan (Dumas's hero), the captain of the king's musketeers.

Fouquet's trial for embezzlement lasted nearly three years. His defense was airtight, and his judges were inclined in his favor, as were also many important persons. Louis hoped for a death sentence, but the best he could get was life imprisonment. Fouquet spent the next nineteen years in the fortress-prison of Pignerol (now Pinerolo, Italy), which France had just acquired. The whole affair was a mighty warning to insolent aristocrats and all other forms of entrenched privilege, especially that of Parlement.

Colbert took over the direction of France's finances in fact, though he was not appointed comptroller general until 1665. His astonishing success in administering that department of government gave him immediate fame. In fact, historians still debate—with some humor—whether Louis XIV made Colbert, or Colbert made Louis XIV.

The principle of Colbert's economic theory would later be called mercantilism. An oversimplified explanation of that term is that the nation which has the most gold (actual cash) in its treasury is the richest. On the surface, this point of view seems self-evident, but wealth (the good of the people) and actual money (gold) should not be confused; they are often mutually antagonistic. Another error in the theory is that the seller of goods—mercantilism emphasizes the importance to a country of its exports exceeding its imports—is always the gainer, while the buyer is the loser. Both parties, however, stand to gain.

Neither Louis XIV nor Colbert would have acknowledged these flaws even if they saw them. Louis wanted all power vested in the strong, central ruler he was determined to be. Colbert willingly provided him with the means for achieving and holding that position. In the seventeenth century the power and prestige of a nation depended on the strength of its army. There was no such thing as a draft, or any sense of patriotism that might induce a man to volunteer for military service in the national army. All soldiers were bought through a complicated and corrupt machinery, and few served for any other reason than the loot they expected to get in campaigning. Ob-

Jean-Baptiste Colbert (1619–83).

viously, therefore, the monarch who had the most gold in his vaults could buy the largest and strongest army—and navy and diplomatic corps as well. By dint of these, he would have the most powerful and prestigious nation.

Foreign trade was the means that Colbert, who belonged to a family of traders, hit upon as the fundamental means of filling Louis XIV's treasury. Money must come in; as little as possible should go out of the country.

To provide materials for the exports that would bring in cash, Colbert devoted himself primarily to the encouragement of domestic industries and the creation of new ones. He was not, however, so dedicated to the acquisition of gold as to forget that "wealth" also consists of natural resources: iron, copper, and lead for weapons and machines; timber for ships; hemp for rope; flax for cloth- and lace-making; horses, vines, and, above all, wheat. Consequently, Colbert subsidized mining and agriculture so that France would have its own sources of supply. Also, he put people to work, particularly in the textile and glass manufactories he established as government enterprises under state patronage. He even imported trained laborers, particularly for the French mines, and invited foreign capital to invest in his manufacturing plants. To expedite the transportation of goods to ports, he developed roads and canals.

From the point of view of an American, Colbert's most important means of enlarging France's power was his development of colonies in the Western Hemisphere that would supply the mother country with produce and would also buy its exports. In 1663, the French outposts in Canada had only 2,500 inhabitants. Ten years later, they numbered 10,000, and Quebec had become an important port. Colbert backed Robert La Salle's expedition of 1682 down the Mississippi River, which gave France a colonial empire—acquired by the United States in the Louisiana Purchase of 1804. He shipped slaves from

Senegal to the French Caribbean colonies, from which the ships returned laden with sugarcane. To profit from this, Colbert built refineries and made sugar one of France's most rewarding exports. Also, France sold its brandy, olive oil, and cloth to its colonies in the Western Hemisphere.

Colbert's attempts to extend French colonization into the Far East, however, were less successful; the English, Dutch, and Portuguese were already too firmly entrenched there.

What Colbert created for France was a planned economy, the successful operation of which made him indispensable to Louis XIV. So many other departments besides the treasury were put under Colbert's supervision that before he died, in 1683, he controlled almost every branch of the government. Even the army was indirectly responsible to him; the navy was not only his special creation but his pride and joy. He increased its 20 ships to 270; the merchant fleet he enlarged from 60 to 700 ships. He passed on his functions to his son, Colbert de Seignelay; his brother Colbert de Croissy; and his nephew Colbert de Torcy.

Work was Colbert's passion, and method his means. He believed that there was nothing that human reason could not accomplish. All his decisions were little more than a careful examination of the data he collected on a subject; the facts made the decision. Yet he was a man of taste, and he patronized artists, writers, and learned institutions.

Everything Colbert did was undertaken for the greater glory of France and the prestige of its king. Louis XIV greatly appreciated Colbert's efforts and achievements. Without them Louis probably never could have realized his grandiose ideals. But Louis never really liked the man; Colbert protested against the king's extravagance and the cost of his court and his wars. The French peasants, artisans, and businessmen hated Colbert, for it was they who suffered most from his reforms which brought France greater prosperity than it had ever known before. Colbert's body had to be buried secretly in order to keep it from desecration by the Paris mobs who rejoiced at his death.

Louis XIV did not intend that merely his domestic ministers should feel the weight of his authority or recognize the *gloire* of the king. All nations were to acknowledge his prestige.

Louis's first brush with a foreign power was the result of a street brawl in London on October 10, 1661. The Spanish ambassador to the Court of Saint James arrived in the English capital with a retinue of several thousand Spanish soldiers from the Spanish Netherlands as his "servants." The French ambassador had only about five hundred when he entered London. In a time when all the rights and trappings of precedence were a matter of personal and national honor, this display on the part of the Spanish ambassador was not appreciated by the French. When the Baron de Vatteville and the Conde d'Estrade went to present their credentials to King Charles II, fighting broke out between the two private armies, and the outnumbered French lost several men.

Hearing of the incident while he was at dinner, Louis XIV gave a remarkable performance of an utterly outraged man. Without consulting Foreign Minister Lionne, Louis ordered the Spanish ambassador to France out of his kingdom, recalled his ambassador from Madrid, canceled all Spanish passports, and demanded punitive action from his cousin Charles II of England.

Louis's father-in-law, Philip IV of Spain, tried to calm him down, but Louis claimed that the incident was due to his having arranged the marriage of Charles II to the well-dowered Portuguese princess Catherine da Braganza, which the Spaniards did not want. Louis would accept nothing less than an abject apology for the insult to French dignity. Philip IV was in no military or financial position to withhold that. Thereafter the French ambassador took precedence at every court in Europe except that of the Austrian emperor in Vienna, to which Louis sent only a minister.*

On August 20, 1662, a similar occurrence took place in Rome, where the Corsican Guards of Pope Alexander VII attacked the Farnese Palace, the headquarters of the French ambassador, the Duc de Créqui. Louis XIV had undoubtedly instructed his ambassador to start this fracas as a protest against the pope's attempts to abolish extraterritoriality in Rome. But when the pope, who had no love for France anyway, delayed the apology that Louis demanded, Louis wrote in his own hand to every Catholic ruler, recommending that they all unite to prevent such an incident reoccurring. Then he captured the papal city of Avignon, in southern France, and threatened to attack Rome with his army. Alexander VII promptly sent his nephew Cardinal Chigi to Paris with a formal apology. Louis subsequently restored Avignon to the pontiff, but the papacy's already dwindling power in European politics suffered a mortal blow.

Charles II of England was not spared his cousin's insistence on French supremacy. Louis insisted that English ships dip their colors to French ones whenever they met at sea. Charles ordered his admirals to do so, but secretly instructed them to avoid any occasion when that deference to France would be necessary.

The crowning triumph of Louis XIV's first year as absolute monarch of France came on November 1, 1661, when Queen Maria Theresa gave birth to a son and heir. Louis was so elated that he forgot his dignity and rushed to a window to

---

* An ambassador, even today, represents the very person of his chief of state. A minister represents only his government.

shout to the expectant crowd: "The queen's had a boy!" With at least one direct successor assured, the policy Louis was constructing seemed indestructible.

Louis's affections had already strayed from his wife to his sister-in-law, and then to one of her ladies-in-waiting. During Maria Theresa's difficult labor, however, he sat by her bed, holding her hand. He was "sensibly penetrated by grief," as one spectator said, adding that there was "no room for doubt that his love for the queen held a greater place in his heart than any other." Poor Maria Theresa was to have four more children, but all of them died in infancy.

To celebrate the birth of a dauphin, Louis XIV held a splendid pageant, which he called a Carrousel, in the gardens of the Tuileries Palace in Paris. (The location is still called Place du Carrousel.) Fifteen thousand people watched what was really a ballet on horseback. Louis appeared in the costume of a Roman emperor, at the head of 400 horsemen. Then came squadrons of "Persians" under his brother, who was dressed as a Persian king; "Turks" under Condé in appropriate costume; bands of "East Indians" and "American Indians" headed by other peers of the realm, each leading a troop of 150 horsemen.

The horses were adorned with ostrich plumes, ribbons, colored blankets, and silver harnesses. All the "Persians" and "Turks" were brandishing scimitars. The "American Indians" had stuffed birds in their headpieces, and their horses' tails were braided with "snakes." There were horse quadrilles, races, and riding with a lance at a ring. (Actual jousting was forbidden, owing to the accidental death of King Henry II in a tournament on July 10, 1559.) Maria Theresa was the queen of the Carrousel, and gave handsome prizes to the winners of the tests of skill. The whole show was so popular that it had to be repeated later in the summer.

It was on that occasion that Louis XIV took the emblem

of the sun as his own, and also the motto *nec pluribus impar* ("superior to everyone").

Louis later explained his choice to his son: "The sun was chosen for the singular quality of the glory that surrounds it; for the light that it lends to other heavenly bodies which make a kind of court around it; for the equality and justice with which it sheds its light on all parts of the earth [Louis was vague about climatology]; for the good it confers everywhere, endlessly producing life, joy, and activity; for its uninterrupted and steady movement [the discoveries of Copernicus and Galileo were not yet accepted by good Catholics], though it seems forever at rest. Hence, it is surely the most vivid and beautiful symbol for a great king."

The motto, Louis wrote, was suggested by "those who saw me ruling with ease and without being defeated by any of the many demands upon me. They thought that . . . since I was equal to so many responsibilities, I would doubtless be capable of governing still more empires. Their appreciation was flattering to a young king's ambition, and I liked it."

Forever after, Louis XIV was to be known as the Sun King.

V

THE TRAPPINGS
OF MAJESTY

The grand party at Nicolas Fouquet's palace gave Louis XIV at least one other idea than the advisability of removing his finance minister from office. He must have a palace of his own whose splendor would dazzle not only France but all the world. Its entertainments would surpass Fouquet's in that they would be continuous. Its etiquette would safeguard every shade of rank and privilege. Because he, the Sun King, would be constantly there, every member of the nobility who wanted anything, from a pension to an office in the government, would have to come there to seek it, for only the king would dispense such favors. Once there, they would be kept in thrall by the beauty of the place and the honor of being close to their god. It was to be the loveliest jail in the world.

Louis disliked Paris both because he was an outdoors man and also because he could never forgive the Parisian mobs for the humiliations they had forced upon him and his mother. He rarely inhabited his palaces in the city, preferring those at Saint-Germain, Fontainebleau, Chambord, and Vincennes, where the hunting was good. Those, however, were extremely old buildings and not in a French style of architecture. Furthermore, they had no landscaping, and one of the aspects of Vaux-le-Vicomte that Louis had most admired was the gardens that André Lenôtre had created for Fouquet. Louis XIV had also been taken by the new architectural style of Louis Le Vau, and the decorative art of Charles Le Brun, which gave Vaux-le-Vicomte a distinctly modern and French flavor.

Louis's father, Louis XIII, as enthusiastic a huntsman as his son, had, in 1624, built a lodge at Versailles, twelve miles from Paris, so that he and his entourage could spend a comfortable night there after a day's hunting in the surrounding forest. It was a relatively simple structure, consisting of a main building with two wings and four pavilions, and it was simply furnished. Probably designed by de Brosse, it was in the old— or Italianate—style of architecture. Louis XIV had been there several times in his youth, and had occasionally used it as his father did.

By the autumn of 1661, Louis had decided that this hunting lodge, called the house of cards, was to be the nucleus of the magnificent cage he would construct for the nobles of his realm whose independence he distrusted. It would also be the frame he required to set off his self-portrait as the greatest king on earth. Construction began immediately under the supervision of Charles Perrault,* who was to be responsible for the work to Colbert.

Why Louis XIV chose that particular site in Versailles is a mystery, for it was in a depression and had no natural view. The land was marshy, and there was no good water supply.

* Perrault is perhaps better known today as the author of *Mother Goose Tales* (1697), containing such familiar stories as Little Red Ridinghood, Cinderella, Hop-o'-My-Thumb, Bluebeard, The Sleeping Beauty, Puss in Boots, and others. In the literary war of the period between the "ancients" and the "moderns," he was the champion of the "moderns." His principal opponent was Nicolas Boileau, mentioned later. Hence, Perrault was an admirable choice for a king who wanted things up-to-date.

Probably he selected it out of a feeling that he should show some respect for his father; hence his plan to leave Louis XIII's hunting lodge relatively intact.

By the spring of 1664, the work of reconstruction was well enough along on the basic structure—an envelope designed by Le Vau, Fouquet's architect, to enclose the original building— for Louis to invite his court there for a three-day pageant, beginning on May 7, which he called "The Pleasures of the Enchanted Isle."

The theme of that pageant was the enchanted island-garden of Alcina, a supernatural personage in Ariosto's poem of romantic chivalry, *Orlando Furioso*, who typifies sensual pleasure and who turns lovers she has captured into beasts when she is tired of them. Perhaps unconsciously, Louis chose this theme to indicate to his nobles the captivity he intended for them in his enchanting new palace.

The first day of the fete was devoted to feats of knightly valor performed in an arena built to hold two hundred people. The king, his brother, and other nobles represented Charlemagne's paladins. Louis, naturally, was Rogero, the hero of the *Orlando Furioso*; the others were Roland, Ogier the Dane, and so on. Their chief display was riding, lance in hand, at full gallop past a stake from which hung several rings, and unhooking one or more of them. The winner received as prize a diamond-encrusted sword and scabbard.

Then there was a lottery for thirty-five of the court ladies, in which every number drawn won a piece of jewelry.

The evening entertainment was an open-air, torchlit ballet of the four seasons—Spring on a Spanish horse, Summer on an elephant, Autumn on a camel, and Winter on a bear—to music composed for the occasion by Lully. Each season had a company of twelve dancers dressed in costumes symbolizing the appropriate time of year. Then Louis's ever-present armed bodyguards held back the guests while stewards, costumed as Abundance, Joy, Cleanliness, and Good Cheer, set up a crescent-shaped table decorated with festoons of flowers and loaded it with delicacies. That banquet lasted until the early hours of the morning.

The next day was devoted to plays and operas and ballets. The banquet that evening was served from an eight-sided table whose centerpiece was a baroque piece of papier-mâché architecture featuring columns, arches, flower garlands, and statues. Music supplied by the king's twenty-four violins was continuous, for Louis XIV loved music.

The climax of the pageant, on the third evening, was the "destruction" of the enchanted island by fireworks, a contemporary engraving of which makes the display that "broke the magic spell' seem stupendous. Such an engraving—and there were plenty made of various aspects of this and other pageants—was widely sold in France and neighboring countries as propaganda for the Sun King's magnificence.

As the mighty palace of Versailles continued to take shape—it was not truly finished until 1711, though considered complete in 1689—it became clear that its parts radiated from a hub, the bedroom of the Sun King himself. In this enormous chamber, facing the marble courtyard and the principal entrance to the palace, Louis was roused by one elaborate ceremony and escorted to bed by another. He usually ate his midday dinner alone at a small table opposite the middle window.

From that symbolically centralized room fan out the great "public apartments," so called because they were the rooms frequented by the court and visitors to it. Behind and above them, and reached by "hidden" doors and "secret" staircases, is a maze of small, intimate, and charming apartments which were for the private use of the royal family and highly

The Marble Court entrance to the palace of Versailles, which Louis XIV's bedroom overlooked.

The palace of Versailles from the gardens.

privileged nobles. In the attics were tiny, stifling hot rooms designed for the use of the less favored courtiers, any one of whom considered himself blessed by the god-king if he were assigned one. Even here a distinction of favor and rank was made by whether or not there was chalked on the door a "for" or merely the name of the person. In the wings were government offices, rooms for government officials, for servants of the king and of his courtiers and officials, and for servants' servants. The palace could house ten thousand persons.

The public apartments epitomize all ideas of grandeur, lavishness, splendor, and gaudy elegance. The floors are of inlaid wood. The walls are sometimes of marble, sometimes of fine woods, sometimes covered with brocade and adorned with gilded gesso decorations. The ceilings are sculptured and gilded, and almost every one displays an allegorical painting in lively colors, many of which are by Le Brun. Huge crystal or bronze chandeliers hang from them. Tall, arched, deeply recessed windows overlook the great entrance courtyard or the gardens and fountains.

The most famous room is the Hall of Mirrors, completed by Jules Hardouin Mansard in 1679, the construction of which unfortunately spoiled the handsomely proportioned façade that Le Vau had designed for the side of the palace facing the gardens. It was intended for balls and for grand ceremonies. Its length of 239 feet, its width of 35 feet, and its height of 42 feet make it probably the most impressive room of its kind in the world. The inner wall consists of marble arches that frame mirrors, which, in Louis XIV's time, were rare and fabulously expensive. The outer wall, overlooking the gardens, contains seventeen high, arched windows. The ceiling paintings by Le Brun were executed between 1679 and 1683 and represent the victories of Louis XIV, and, in the center, Louis governing the kingdom of France alone.

The fault in the palace is that it lacks restraint. It is, as it was designed to be, a vulgar display of the pomp and circumstance of the egocentric individual who ordered it. The decorations, almost all of which feature Louis as a person rather than as an institution, are cold and shallow. The only masterpieces of design and execution are the splendid stairways and perhaps the chapel, which was the last part of the palace to be constructed.

The same unfavorable criticism cannot be made of the landscaping of the palace park. Lenôtre, who designed it all, took as his principle an easy transition for the eye from the art of the palace to the nature of the surrounding countryside. One looks down long vistas framed by trees and adorned with urns and statues to the Grand Canal on the horizon.

There were some flower beds, but the emphasis was on trees, fountains, and walks. The fountains are generally huge basins of water, in the center of which is a piece of allegorical sculpture, sometimes ringed with smalled pieces. High jets of water spurt upward from the basin and also across it to make a splendid show. Trees were brought to Versailles from all over France; and there was an orangery of a thousand orange trees, which Louis XIV appropriated from Fouquet. (These were his favorite plants, and he kept some in silver tubs in all his rooms.) The broad lawns, the avenues, and the paths were laid out in an orderly, symmetrical fashion, and almost all were varied with a surprise—an amusing statue, a little temple, or an artificial grotto. In 1668, a zoo was added.

Louis adored these gardens and may have been personally responsible for much of their beauty. It is known that he conferred regularly with Le Vau and Lenôtre, and later with Mansard, who was almost an intimate friend; but whether he dictated his own ideas to them or merely approved their plans is not certain. He was a man of little artistic discrimination, but he had the good sense to choose reliable subordinates both in statecraft and in artistic matters.

The cost of Versailles, and of the two smaller pleasure palaces that Louis built nearby at Marly and Trianon, was, of course, tremendous. The palace and the park of Versailles came to the equivalent of over $500,000,000. Marly cost about $200,000,000. Thirty-six thousand workmen were laboring at Versailles by 1685, and six thousand horses. Many of these workmen died of malaria there, particularly while constructing the necessary waterworks.

Such expenditure of money—and of human life—meant nothing to Louis XIV so long as it contributed to his prestige. Even Colbert, who fumed at the drains it put on his treasury, approved in principle. That Versailles did impress rival nations is proved by the number of replicas built by other monarchs in Vienna, Potsdam, Munich, Dresden, Stockholm, Copenhagen, and St. Petersburg (Leningrad). Most of these, because they are smaller, are more tasteful than Versailles.

In 1668, Louis moved his household, his court, and his councils to Versailles, even though only the central—or envelope—portion of the palace was finished. Building was going on all around, and the noise and the continual moving of furniture and works of art—called the *brouhaha* of Versailles— were distracting.

The palace was uncomfortable in many other ways. It was freezing cold in winter and broiling hot in summer, for Louis forbade tall enough chimneys to draw well lest they mar the external proportions of the building, and he also forbade shutters at the windows for the same reason. There were no indoor toilet facilities. Courtiers who were not housed in the then small palace had to take exorbitantly priced lodgings in the nearby village and scrounge for their meals. Worst of all, they had to stand during most of the long day at court,

The Hall of Mirrors, Versailles.

for only the most highly privileged had the right to sit—on an armchair, on a straight chair, or on an upholstered stool, according to their rank—unless they were playing cards.

The court entertainments, generally on three evenings a week, were what might be called "at homes," and lasted from 7:00 to 10:00 P.M. Attendance was practically compulsory, for if the king could spare the time from government business to favor his court with his company and noticed that anyone was absent—as he was quite capable of doing—the absentee might as well retire from court. Most nobles considered exile from Versailles equivalent to exile from their country. Those who preferred their own châteaus or could not afford to live at court were regarded as bumpkins.

The evening opened with a concert, after which a certain informality prevailed as everyone fell to playing cards or billiards. The king, who often took a cue, was a good player— also a good sport if he lost. There was frantic gambling, and cheating, at the card tables, where the most popular game was a forerunner of Twenty-one. An early form of roulette was also popular; it was crooked. Queen Maria Theresa was a passionate gambler and a constant loser. Louis, however, seldom played cards; he did not like to sit still so long. Sometimes in the summer the gambling was exchanged for boating parties in gondolas on the Grand Canal.

On the other evenings of the week there were theatrical entertainments. At these, at least, one could sit, and, as Mme de Sévigné remarked, they cost nothing. For the cost of living at Versailles was staggering; some nobles had to apply to the king for an allowance to support themselves there, which he would give if he really wanted the applicant to remain at court. The chief expense was clothes, for the king insisted on elaborate dress.

The etiquette at Louis XIV's court was formal and rigid

and grew more so as the king advanced in years. Louis's sense of humor was limited to an appreciation of practical jokes, but the prankster had to be careful not to go beyond the king's notions of what was dignified. Louis assumed so great a dignity that he inspired terror. He could also be cruel; he once had an old woman whipped because she screamed insults at him after her only son had been killed in a fall from a scaffolding at Versailles, where he had been a laborer. And there was the famous Man in the Iron Mask (which was actually made of black velvet) whom Louis kept imprisoned for life; no one else knew his identity or his crime. Louis was not only a jailer; he had some of the traits of an unimaginative schoolteacher.

All in all, life at the court of Versailles was as vexatious and boring as life in an "organization man" complex of today. But it was the only way of getting on in the world of Louis XIV.

The Sun King's contributions to the development of the arts were limited to those he personally enjoyed—the dance, music, and the drama. Because he was a good dancer himself, he encouraged dancing as a social pastime. The dances, however, were designed to display not only Louis's skill but his dignity. Hence, they lost the spontaneity and freedom of physical movement they had in an earlier period and became as rigid in style as the rest of court activities. Technical perfection, regularity, balance, and restraint were the criteria. Louis's dancing master, Charles Beauchamp, prescribed rules that the court obediently followed under the impression that they were being creative in transforming what were once lively dances of the people into the stately minuet and gavotte. Close movement, small steps, formalized bows or curtsies, and the mere touching of hands between partners made these courtly dances disciplined rituals.

Ballet left the palace dance floor, where it had been a kind of carefree charade, and ascended the stage as allegorical extravaganzas. Courtiers still took part, however, and Louis himself loved to impersonate the sun god Apollo. (Various representations of the sun are common decorative motifs in the palace of Versailles.) Professional dancers were added to the amateurs, and in 1661, Louis XIV approved the founding of an academy to train them both to perform and to teach.

The dancing itself consisted of elegant body posturing and small movement. There was no lightness or elasticity; the elaborate costumes alone would have seriously hampered, if not prevented, any emphasis on those now admired qualities. To accomplish them, the basic five positions of the feet were invented. There would be no attempt to express emotion or to interpret a story in stage dancing for another hundred years. In fact, the character of all the artwork of the age seems to have progressed from this confinement of the spontaneous release of feelings, which dancing basically is, into a codified, imitative ritual. To learn to dance was essential to social success; it meant learning to be artificial.

Ballet, as Louis XIV enjoyed it, has long vanished from the scene except for the music composed for the court dances. Indeed, we tend today to think of a minuet, gavotte, polonaise, allemande, or bourrée less as a dance than as a name for a musical composition.

Louis XIV's highly favored court composer was Jean Baptiste Lully, a Florentine by birth. Lully, an excellent violinist and dancer himself, was twenty years old when he entered the king's service, and for the remaining thirty-five years of his life he composed and conducted an extraordinary amount of dance, ballet, and opera music. Out of Italian models he created a national French operatic style, particularly by inventing the French overture, and disciplined his singers

Molière (Jean Baptiste Poquelin) (1622–73), by Pierre Mignard.
Musée de Chantilly.

to follow the score as written. Lully had considerable influence on composers of other nations, especially on the English Henry Purcell; most of these composers gave Lully's rather superficial style more emotional honesty and depth.

Lully frequently collaborated on a court spectacle with Molière (Jean Baptiste Poquelin), Louis XIV's favorite dramatist and one of the greatest of all playwrights. Like most great humorists, Molière had a life that was a tragedy of poor health, disappointment, and deception. Perhaps he never realized all his gifts, for Louis took him under his patronage in 1665 and made him spend much of his time devising court entertainments, most of which were vapid. In spite of that obligation, Molière produced at least four masterpieces: *Tartuffe* (1664), *Don Juan* (1665), *Le Misanthrope* (1666), and *L'Avare* (The Miser) (1668). Somewhat less profound studies of human nature and society, but brilliant pieces of humor, are *Le Médecin malgré lui* (The Doctor in Spite of Himself), *Le Malade imaginaire* (The Hypochondriac), *Le Bourgeois gentilhomme* (The Would-be Gentleman), *L'École des femmes* (The School for Wives), and *Amphitryon*. He is credited with thirty-two plays in all.

Molière's situations and plots tend to be conventional and sometimes artificial, and they are often resolved by an unmotivated trick. The plays in general deal with the difficulties of young lovers whose happiness is threatened by the interference of their stupid or bigoted elders. Molière had little faith in anyone over thirty.

Often these difficulties are straightened out by the earthy common sense of a character of a lower stratum of society, usually an outspoken servant. Molière's sharp satire of the society of his time is directed at the pomposity and pretentiousness of the lesser nobility and the rising merchant class, who have lost touch with reality.

Those levels of society were considered fit subjects for comedy; Molière wrote no tragedies—in the literary sense of that term—for tragedy was then concerned only with royal personages who were represented with superhuman or ideal endowments marred by a fatal human weakness. Molière saw all humanity as fatally weak, sometimes so sympathetically that his plays are "black" comedies, defining the true tragedy of the human condition. Even his most boisterous farces show his pity for the victims who have invited their own discomfort.

Molière's major characters are types. The construction of a "character" was popular in his time; its success depended upon the writer's skill in blending the predominant traits of many individuals into a plausible and recognizable composite—the absentminded man, for example, or the gossip, or the vain person, or the self-righteous one. Just as a real human being can allow a vagary or a prejudice to dominate his behavior to the point of his appearing ridiculous, so Molière's characters lose their standing in society by failing to observe a sense of proportion—one of the bases of all humor.

Molière's great art lies in his ability to make his types real, consisting of many more dimensions than appear on the surface. He is a profound psychologist, noting how a person's stress on one aspect of life cannot help repressing other feelings. He devises means by which subordinate characters in his plays reveal to the audience—and eventually to the principal character himself—what those repressed feelings are and how essential it is to personal happiness that they be given some expression.

Molière's major plays also deal with fundamental problems of morality. Perhaps the most basic one is whether the pursuit of an abstract ideal—that is, one not a projection of a human being's own personality—is beneficial or harmful. In *Tartuffe*, for example, Orgon decides to dedicate himself, his family, and his money to religion, which he has just discovered in the person of a hypocrite and swindler, Tartuffe. In *Le Misanthrope*, Alceste decides that he must cultivate utter honesty and truth, and will have nothing to do with persons who compromise it. In *L'Avare*, Harpagon persuades himself that the power of wealth is an end in itself. And in *Don Juan*, Don Juan finds the gratification of the senses more appealing than considerations of conscience.

In spite of the trick endings which Molière designed to persuade an audience that responsibility to other human beings is the better way, he leaves an anxious question—Is conventional morality a harmful superstition or a necessary and beneficial directive toward individual happiness?

It is a great pity that none of Molière's plays has been truly well translated into English—or, for that matter, adequately performed on the American stage. Too often, American productions turn the peaks of the high comedy he reached into buffoonery and horseplay. In France, Molière's masterpieces are still performed more frequently than the works of any other playwright. He is the master map to the labyrinth of the French national character.

Louis XIV also admired and patronized a writer of superb tragedies, Jean Racine, who, in 1670, supplanted his equally great but then aging predecessor, Pierre Corneille. Corneille's tragedies properly belong to the period of Louis XIII, but Louis XIV knew them well and may have been deeply influenced by them. Louis's decision to resign his love for Marie Mancini in favor of national interests seems to have been based on Corneille's morality that love must be sacrificed to duty. Racine's more realistic attitude is that man is the helpless victim of love. A contemporary critic, La Bruyère, said that Corneille represented human beings as they ought to be; Racine showed them as they are.

Jean Baptiste Racine (1639–99).

Racine's subject matter, as was customary for French tragedy in the seventeenth century, is derived from Greek and Roman sources. His masterpiece *Phèdre*, for example, is based on a tragedy of Euripides; another, *Andromaque*, on an episode of the Trojan War; a third, *Britannicus*, on an incident in the reign of Nero. Two fine tragedies of Racine's, *Athalie* and *Esther*, are dramatizations of Old Testament conflicts. (*Athalie* from II Chronicles 22-23; *Esther* from the book of that name.) All Racine's major characters are of the highest social orders, most of them royalty, and their emotions are suited to the grandeur of their positions. For all the truth in La Bruyère's remark, Racine is not concerned with the everyday citizen of seventeenth-century France, but with monumental figures from a supposedly heroic and certainly long-gone past.

To Racine, Venus, the goddess of love, rules human destinies. Hence, his greatest figures are women—noble, savage, ruthless, and irresistible. Men are helpless in their clutches, for women represent the force of love in human affairs. Perhaps Racine's women betray their men unwillingly into cowardice and crime, but the experience makes its ruinous conclusion seem worthwhile. But Racine could also create an inspiring woman, Esther, or one, Andromaque, whose courage in her pathetic helplessness makes her tower above the men who control her fate.

Racine's lines are as effective as Shakespeare's in adding emotional depth to the predicaments of his characters. More than a mere playwright, he was a great poet. Both he and Shakespeare could transform a bare stage into a forest or a raging sea by the power of their words over the imagination of their audience. Racine's poetry has a grand sound to it that makes the grandeur of his characters' passions almost intolerable.

Witnessing a well-acted production of a tragedy by Racine

is an exhausting emotional experience, for the dramatic conventions of the time permitted no comic interlude, as in Shakespeare's tragedies, to relieve the tension. Unfortunately there is no adequate translation into English of Racine's works, and few if any currently active American dramatic artists are of sufficient stature to portray his roles, almost every one of which might be called a combination of King Lear and Lady Macbeth.

Louis XIV undoubtedly got many ideas from acting his part as the greatest king on earth from watching Racine's tragedies.

Many other excellent writers of the period—probably the grandest in the annals of French literature—Louis XIV did not directly patronize. Jean de La Fontaine, for example, was politically displeasing to the king. François, Duc de La Rochefoucauld, was out of the royal favor for having sided with the nobles during the Second War of the Fronde. Jean de La Bruyère was a protégé of the Prince de Condé. But Louis did support Nicolas Boileau, a first-rate poet and critic, whose later work the king corrupted into fulsome flattery of his own royal achievements. Boileau's earlier work is a model of stylistic elegance, and it did much to elevate the standards of French poetical taste, but it has little more than historical interest for the twentieth-century American reader.

La Fontaine's *Fables*, however, have been a joy since they began appearing in 1668. Beautifully rendered into English by the American poet Marianne Moore, they have recently become available to every American, who should learn to treasure them as the French have done. La Fontaine had a wry and ribald humor that makes the animal characters of his fables devastating satires on the human beings who think themselves higher and nobler than the beasts. For every animal in the fables is really a man or a woman dressed up in fur or plumage, and superficially bizarre situations in the animal world become, in La Fontaine's sprightly verse, everyday occurrences in human life.

The *Maximes* of the Duc de La Rochefoucauld are shrewd observations on the motives of human behavior. Brittle, cynical, witty—and perhaps superficial—they are still an excellent guide for anyone who wishes to avoid seeming smug.

Even such a brief survey of the literature of Louis XIV's reign would be incomplete without a mention of the *Caractères* of La Bruyère, the nature of which has been suggested previously; Mme de La Fayette's fine psychological novel, *La Princesse de Clèves*; and the sparkling letters of Mme de Sévigné. For precision, perception, and elegance, the fine literary works of the period have never been surpassed.

Not so much can be said for other areas of the arts under Louis XIV. Works of painting and sculpture were almost wholly "official"; that is, dictated as to content and style by the king and the nobles, without whose patronage the artists could barely survive. As might be expected, the style was flamboyant and in the grand manner. The subject matter, generally portraits, was idealized—hence, prettified or apostrophized. King and courtiers were frequently portrayed as divinities of classical mythology or as heroes of ancient Roman history. Occasionally the artist's brilliance of technique saves these representations from being absurd, as in Charles Le Brun's splendid portrait of Chancellor Pierre Séguier (in the Louvre, Paris) or Hyacinthe Rigaud's portraits of Jacques Bossuet and Louis XIV (also in the Louvre). Rigaud was probably the best of the court painters; he was able to combine some psychological interpretation of his subject and honesty of representation with artificial grandeur, and his canvases have a truly regal quality.

To the modern eye, far more interesting painters are the

brothers Le Nain (Louis, Antoine, and Mathieu), who specialized in humble peasants and simple rural scenes which they rendered with honest sympathy and dignity. A fine painter who flourished before Louis XIV took over the government in 1661 was Georges de La Tour, whose sincerely intense and dramatic religious scenes are peopled with ordinary folk. Neither of those first-rate artists received royal patronage, nor did Claude Lorrain (Gellée) and the master painter Nicolas Poussin, Frenchmen of the era who worked principally in Italy. Antoine Watteau's wistfully charming, tragicomic paintings of actors, musicians, and gay courtiers in rustic settings belong to the last years of Louis XIV's reign, when the Sun King's glory had faded into a pensive twilight.

Official sculpture was even more stiff and artificial than painting. Away from the stultifying dictatorship of Versailles, however, flourished such strong and dynamic sculptors as Pierre Puget, whose best work is in Toulon and Marseilles, and Guillaume Coustou, whose splendid "Horses of Marly" now flank the entrance to the Champs Élysées in Paris's Place de la Concorde.

The most typical of Louis XIV's court sculptors was Antoine Coysevox, an imitator of the far greater Giovanni Lorenzo Bernini. Bernini had been imported from Rome to Paris to renovate the Louvre, but he behaved in an insufferably arrogant fashion and went home in disgust after Colbert had criticized his plans for not providing the palace with enough sanitation facilities. Bernini left behind a glorious but highly idealized portrait bust of Louis XIV, now in the palace of Versailles, which epitomizes all the morning glitter of the Sun King and the early days of his reign.

Bernini's departure made the reconstruction of the Louvre available to Charles Perrault, who designed a colonnade for the palace's eastern façade that is a true masterpiece. Other fine examples of the baroque architecture of the period are the chapel of Val-de-Grace; Libéral Bruant and Mansard's church of Saint-Louis-des-Invalides (adjoining the Hôtel des Invalides); and, in city planning, the Place Vendôme, the Tuileries gardens, and the Avenue des Champs-Élysées—all in Paris.

Colbert managed to convince Louis XIV that, much as the latter disliked Paris, he should not let his magnificence be blemished by a substandard capital. While Paris remained a filthy, stinking, dark, overcrowded, and pestilential city for another two hundred years, Louis did vastly improve its surface appearance with renovations and new construction— wide streets, broad boulevards, squares and parks, as well as buildings and monuments. He also gave the capital a semblance of law and order under his able police commissioner, Nicolas de La Reynie.

Colbert's encouragement of French industry to provide articles for export stimulated the manufacture of tapestries. After he put the factories at Aubusson, Beauvais, and of the Gobelin family at Rheims under royal control, they produced magnificent wall decorations. The Gobelins' factory also manufactured textiles, woodwork, silver- and other metalwork, and marble inlay. Fine carpets came from another government-subsidized plant, La Savonnerie; and exquisite porcelains came from state-controlled factories at Rouen and St.-Cloud. Furniture for the royal palaces was often of silver or fine wood encrusted with silver, gold, and ormolu. Most of that has been melted down, but many pieces survive from the workshop of André Charles Boulle; these are gorgeously carved, adorned with scrolls of ormolu, and inlaid with tortoiseshell and mother-of-pearl. The minor arts of decoration were, on the whole, more tasteful and better executed than the major ones.

The unity of French civilization that Louis XIV determined to achieve through the centralization of administration affected even so usually individualized a dimension of a nation's culture as the arts. No matter how many different forms it took, one spirit animated the various creators—a profound belief in and reverence for one supreme power. Man and his world are seen as totally earthbound, separated by an enormous gulf of empty space from the controllers above. Hence the weightiness—the downward pull, as it were—of the works of the age. The light, mocking laughter of a Molière, a La Fontaine, a La Rochefoucauld, a Sévigné, or a Watteau seems irrelevant, if not sacrilegious. Yet it is this undertone that redeems the period for the modern mind. The details of the wars, the treaties, the internal politics, the religious controversies, have faded almost beyond the perception of non-specialized eyes. But even the little touches of the artists still shine undimmed to attest the glory and magnificence of the Age of Louis XIV.

VI

LOUIS THE GREAT

Versailles would take a long time to reach perfection, and it would be an even longer time before reports of its magnificence would impress other lands with the power and the glory of Louis XIV. In the meantime, the only way by which that impression could be made was war.

War was not only the most effective means, it was the way the seventeenth century expected and highly approved. There could be no *gloire* without war for either an individual or a nation. War and the Church—the red and the black—were the only acceptable careers for a man of noble instincts, and such a man began preparing for his career as a soldier in his childhood games. During the unwelcome periods of peace he kept in practice by participating in the warlike displays that were the basis of such entertainments as the Carrousel or the Pleasures of the Enchanted Isle.

Once Colbert had put the finances of France into sufficient order for the once empty treasury to show signs of becoming an ever-flowing source of supply for an invincible army, Louis XIV looked toward the immediate realization of his ambitions. And while Colbert had been filling the royal coffers with gold,

Le Tellier and Louvois had been steadily creating a war machine by improving the quality of the French king's fighting forces and the efficiency of their management.

In 1661, the "king's army" was a joke. The king was, as it were, merely one of several partners in a military corporation. He controlled only a certain number of regiments and their colonels; the others were loyal to one or another of the other partners. These were the colonel-generals of the infantry, the cavalry, and the artillery. They had bought their post for a huge sum; it was very definitely their property, and they consulted the war secretary about the management of it only when it was to their advantage to do so. Once an army was in the field, the government had almost no control over it.

An army officer invested in the military corporation by buying a commission. He did not necessarily purchase this from the king; more often he paid one of the other partners for it. He then recovered his investment by selling subordinate commissions to captains. Each of these guaranteed to recruit the hundred soldiers necessary to fill the company for which he was responsible, feed them, and equip them. The state paid those soldiers through the captain, who pocketed the difference between the sum he demanded and the amount he paid out to his men.

A captain frequently reported a full company when he actually had only, say, fifty men. How else would he make a profit on his investment? If one of the infrequent government inspections of the troops was imminent, the captain borrowed the "missing" men from another company or hired extras until the inspection was over. Since there were no uniforms or any official muster rolls, this deception was hard to detect. Furthermore, most of the partners' inspectors were lenient; otherwise there might be no company at all. Half a company on hand was better than none.

This practice, of course, meant that a commander rarely if ever knew for certain how many men he could put into an action. Conversely, he seldom knew how many of those who actually participated in an engagement survived it in fighting condition. A captain, in order to increase the return on his investment, might report thirty or forty men killed, whereas he had truly lost none.

The common soldier generally came from the dregs of society. Many were kidnapped from the slums of Paris or other cities. Those who enlisted had no other objective than the plunder they hoped to get or the money civilians paid them to be spared their depredations. They deserted if they were not paid, as often happened, or if the campaign were too un-successful to provide them with loot. The only discipline was an unannounced wholesale hanging as an occasional warning. The officers were often no more safe from their men than the hapless inhabitants of an invaded country.

In 1666, when Louis XIV was seriously preparing for his first major war, Le Tellier yielded, for practical purposes, his office of war minister to his son Louvois. Le Tellier sub-sequently became chancellor of France. Louvois put into effect the many reforms his father had initiated in the corrupt and inefficient army and also advanced the work of organization.

Consequently, for the sake of convenience, Louvois can be regarded as the real father of the French army system which lasted until Napoleon revised it around 1800. Louvois was a hard worker and a clear thinker, but brutal and, needless to say, a warmonger. As great an administrator as Colbert, who fre-quently opposed his plans and methods, Louvois had the ad-vantage of Louis XIV's unswerving admiration and support.

A stroke of luck for Louvois was the death, in 1662, of the Duc d'Epernon, colonel-general of the infantry and one of the "partners." Louvois handed Epernon's post—and share in the

François Michel Le Tellier, Marquis de Louvois (1641–91), by Pierre Mignard.

corporation—to Louis XIV, thus bringing all infantry officers under the king's jurisdiction. The power of the other partners was, therefore, considerably weaknened, and Louis hammered away at it until their posts became nonfunctional. The army thus eventually became as centralized as the other branches of the government.

Louis found his new duties as virtual commander in chief very agreeable. He liked paper work, and he preferred a desk job to a command in the field. His meticulous attention to details made him a good administrator, but his directives to his generals, often written from miles behind the lines, infuriated those men who were on the field and thus knew better than the king what could or could not be accomplished. So long as this finickiness of Louis's was limited to the supervision of maneuvers—the greater part of the army's action—the generals willingly let Louis play at being a military genius. Eventually, however, they—and Louvois—learned to let Louis think he was directing a battle, but acted out of their own military instincts and experience. Louis XIV never could see the campaign for the campsites.

Louvois next attacked the corruption of the subordinate officers by introducing ranks under those which had been purchased and could not, therefore, be taken away from their owners. The new lieutenant colonels, majors, and brigadiers got their posts by appointment on the basis of experience and merit. These new men took over the actual control—but not the ownership—of the regiments and were held responsible for discipline, training, and administration of them. The introduction of these ranks made it possible for a capable man, however poor or humble, to rise in the army, and thus provided an incentive for military service nobler than plunder. The control of the army by nobles alone grew less and less as rankers moved into the officer corps.

Possibly the best known of this new cadre of officers was one Martinet. His first name and his dates have faded from the records, but his last name has become a word in several languages for an uncompromising drillmaster. He also gave his name (in the French language) to the cat-o'-nine-tails, which he is said to have invented. In addition to bringing discipline into the army, Martinet was also an imaginative engineer; it was he who devised the bridge of copper pontoons over which Condé led the French army across the Rhine in 1672. "A man of rare merit and firmness," as Louvois styled him, Martinet, however, never rose higher than a lieutenant colonelcy. He was, nevertheless, a proof of Louvois's ability to make his administration effective by selecting excellent subordinates.

Louvois also checked the practice of padding out a company by ordering surprise inspections and inflicting heavy penalties on captains who failed to produce a number of soldiers equal to that on their report. The captains' payrolls were now audited by the government. Eventually Louvois managed to reduce desertions by fixing a uniform rate of pay and actually paying it, and by insisting on the wearing of uniforms, but the compulsory use of such identification, except for officers, he had to leave to individual colonels.

Louvois saw that a continual flow of young, well-trained blood into the officer corps was essential to a vigorous chain of command. Formerly, a young officer candidate was simply entered in a regiment to learn warfare by whatever means he could—usually pernicious—until the legal red tape of his buying a commission was unraveled. This custom was replaced by nine training schools which cadets were compelled to attend in order to qualify for a commission. There they learned drill, the manual of arms, musketry, mathematics, geography, fencing, riding, and dancing.

Recruits were improved in quality and status. Men now enlisted for a four-year hitch. They had to be in good physical condition, and single, and under forty years of age. France, however, did not have the manpower always to meet these qualifications as Louis XIV's wars increased in number and duration. But the new conditions of pay, service, and care of the wounded attracted soldiers from other countries. By 1679, France could put 280,000 men into the field—more than one-tenth of its population.

Louvois, however, had a streak of the disinclination to try anything new that characterizes many desk generals. He insisted, for example, on retaining the clumsy musket and the pike as infantry weapons long after the more efficient flintlock and the bayonet had rendered them obsolete. He also thought that a mere order was sufficient to effect discipline in the ranks. But as an administrator he excelled. He was ruthless in pursuing corruption and in punishing it when discovered. Field hospitals, for example, which operated by contractors, were greatly improved through Louvois's investigations of dishonesty in their management.

Louvois's greatest administrative triumph was the simple invention of supply dumps and depots for fodder so that the French army did not have to retire from the field in October and wait until the grass was green so that the army animals could be fed, and for the soldiers' rations. The army that could stay in the field the longest, and return to it from winter quarters the earliest, had a great strategic advantage.

Aside, perhaps, from the generals themselves, the most valuable member of Louvois's military staff was Sebastien de Vauban. A superb engineer, Vauban so perfected the methods of fortifying a town and attacking one that it was said: "A town besieged by Vauban is a town captured; a town defended by Vauban is impregnable."

Sebastien Le Prestre, Seigneur de Vauban (1633–1707), by Hyacinthe Rigaud.

Since a campaign consisted almost entirely in taking the enemy's fortresses—pitched battles were not very common until the eighteenth century—Vauban's skills contributed greatly to Louis XIV's military successes. Vauban's calculation of the time it would take for a besieged fortress to surrender was so precise that the moment of capitulation could be prepared for as if it were the arrival of a dignitary on a scheduled airplane flight today. The ladies of the court would be invited to watch the final assault, which was performed to the music of Louis XIV's string orchestra.

Vauban's dream was a line of fortresses along all the frontiers of France—in those days a far more practical defense than the Maginot Line of the late 1930's. Louvois encouraged him to spare no expense in creating these works of military art composed of double and sometimes triple rings of walls, built of stone over earthwork on steep slopes surrounded by deep ditches and bristling with angles. Within those walls were utilitarian low stone buildings with deep cellars. (New York State's Fort Ticonderoga, between Lake George and Lake Champlain, is a good example of this type of fortress, though built after Vauban's death.) Vauban also invented the bayonet, and ricochet batteries.

One of the most important elements of the remodeled French army appears to have been thought up by Louis XIV himself. After the end of the war with Spain in 1659, he decided to reward the demobilized officers, who had no profession other than war, by keeping them on pay as reservists— "thereby," as Louis wrote, "having the means available to mobilize new units in next to no time."

With this new, efficient military machine at his disposal, and with—thanks to Colbert—the money to operate it, Louis was eager to get on with the principal business of a great king, namely, to wage aggressive warfare successfully. It was also time for him to extend France to what he considered its natural boundaries—the Rhine, the Alps, the Pyrenees, and the sea.

Of these "natural boundaries" the Rhine River was by all means the most important because it was the great commercial waterway into the heart of Europe. Louis was less interested in an artistically logical rearrangement of the map of Europe than in acquiring a share of the enormous trade that control of at least one bank of the Rhine would bring him.

Between the "artificial" northeastern boundary of France and the fruitful river, however, lay the independent United Provinces (Holland) and the Spanish Netherlands (Belgium), then also called by the geographical term Flanders. Both areas were among the richest in Europe because of their foreign and domestic trade.

Furthermore, the Spanish Netherlands was a political threat to France. Spain had for centuries been hostile to France, and at the moment was only temporarily pacified. Spain could easily mount an invasion of France from its possessions in Flanders—far more easily than by sending an army over the Pyrenees, or in ships. That northeastern region of Europe is as flat as a floor, which is one reason why it has been a battleground for about one thousand years.

Since 1661, Louis XIV's foreign minister Lionne had pursued a predatory diplomatic policy which had virtually isolated Spain from allies. Louis had been waiting for a good opportunity to put teeth into Lionne's designs. The chance came with the death of King Philip IV of Spain on September 16, 1665.

Philip's will left all his lands to his four-year-old son by his second wife. This sickly baby, who was now King Charles

II of Spain, was not expected to live very long; the fact that he did survive for thirty-five more years greatly complicated European politics.

Laurent Duhan, the secretary of General Turenne, who had long insisted on a French conquest of the Spanish Netherlands, provided Louis XIV with an excellent pretext for a war of aggression—the discovery that, according to an ancient Flemish (*not* Spanish) law, the Spanish Netherlands should be the inheritance of Philip IV's eldest child by his first marriage. The heir to Flanders was, therefore, none other than Louis XIV's wife. It clearly behooved Louis to protect this inheritance of Queen Maria Theresa by the "right of devolution [transference to a successor]," however dubious that law was. Flemish laws had ceased to be effective with the annexation of Flanders by Spain years before.

On May 24, 1667, Turenne, therefore, led the 55,000-strong French army, admirably provisioned by Louvois—even to silverware for the officers' mess—into Flanders. The Spanish forces of 20,000 men retreated, abandoning one after another of their fortresses.

In July, Louis, who had been following Turenne's "promenade" through Flanders, returned to Versailles to pick up his court and take it along with him back to the front. He wanted his new Flemish subjects to see their rightful queen, and he also wanted to impress upon Europe that his was the most powerful kingdom in the world.

Louis's tent was made entirely of Chinese silk; it contained a sleeping room, three salons, and two offices. An observer wrote home to a friend: "All that you have heard of the magnificence of Solomon and the grandeur of the king of Persia does not equal the pomp displayed on this trip . . . plumes, gold embroidery, chariots, mules superbly harnessed, parade horses with equipment embossed in gold . . . the courtiers, the officers, the volunteers—all are sumptuously equipped." The discomforts of such regal campaigning, however, were excessive, especially for the women of the court whose presence Louis required.

War was still a gentleman's game. The loss of life and the bloodshed it entailed offended seventeenth-century mores no more than the mortal accidents that occur in the automoble races, the boxing rings, or even amateur athletic contests, disturb today's sports enthusiasts. Generals were infallibly polite to their adversaries. The commander of an enemy town under siege, for example, kept Louis XIV regularly supplied with ice throughout a long hot summer's assault.

By September, the French army was at the gates of Ghent and Brussels. However, this merry blitzkrieg roused the hostility of the Dutch, who were Louis's allies but who did not want the French as their next-door neighbors in Flanders. It also antagonized the English, with whom Louis was technically at war and who regarded the Spanish Netherlands as England's "natural" boundary. Alarmed by the possible coalition against him, Louis consented to a truce.

The coalition proceeded, however, and a treaty made without Louis's knowledge united England, Holland, and Sweden into the Triple Alliance. These three powers offered to persuade Spain to grant Louis some territory in Flanders. They also secretly agreed to make war on France and reestablish the former frontiers if Louis rejected their proposals.

These reactions caused Louis to invade Franche-Comté, the region of the present Department of Côte d'Or, which was then a dependency of Spain. The attack, led by Condé, came as a complete surprise, for it began on February 4, 1668, a time when every army was supposed to be in winter quarters. By February 13, the entire region was in Louis's hands. His eastern boundary had been extended to the Swiss Alps, and he had prevented Spain from attacking France from Franche-Comté and also from sending aid to the Spanish Netherlands.

Spain was willing to treat for peace, and Louis consented to deal with the Spaniards, even though he was in a very strong position to push his conquests farther. Doubtless he remembered Mazarin's warnings about the danger of a coalition and so decided to be agreeable now and get what he wanted later. The treaty of Aix-la-Chapelle, signed on May 2, 1668, gave Franche-Comté back to Spain, but left Louis in possession of seven important fortified towns in Flanders.

As for getting what he wanted later, Louis made a secret treaty with Emperor Leopold of Austria that, on the still expected early death of Charles II of Spain, France would get all of Franche-Comté and the Spanish Netherlands as well as Sicily, the Philippine Islands, and Spanish North Africa. This Treaty of Partition would have given Louis XIV an empire equal to Charlemagne's and humbled the Hapsburgs to the Bourbons. Louis XIV's high hopes of that eventuality, however, were to end with his France on the brink of disaster.

Louis had not yet reached the Rhine. The United Provinces still stood in the way of his desired territorial expansion. In addition, Dutch foreign trade was an obstacle to Colbert's designs for the expansion of French commerce. Furthermore, Louis regarded the coalition started by the Dutch, whom he had feebly aided in their war with England, as an insolent affront to his *gloire*. He now prepared to humble the Dutch Republic. But he had to wait for four years so that Louvois could continue strengthening the army, Colbert could find money, and Lionne (and after his death in 1671, his successor, Simon Pomponne) could find allies.

On June 1, 1670, a treaty of alliance had been made between France and England, thanks to Lionne's brilliant idea of sending Louis's sister-in-law Henriette to negotiate it with her

Henri de La Tour d'Auvergne, Vicomte de Turenne (1611–75), by Robert Nanteuil.

brother, King Charles II of England. Colbert bought off the king of Sweden, thus ending the Triple Alliance, and also the Emperor Leopold and various German princes. And by February, 1672, Louvois had raised the army to a total of 120,-000 well-equipped soldiers.

The Dutch inquired whether that mighty force was to be used against them, and if so, why. Louis replied that he would make whatever use of his army his dignity required and that he owed no one any further explanation than that.

On March 28, 1672, Louis XIV went to war against the Dutch with no formal declaration of hostilities except a phrase buried in a memorandum which accused them of "ingratitude and insufferable pride."

The French army, under Turenne and Condé, advanced into Holland with little opposition from the Dutch army under William of Orange. The Dutch forces numbered only 55,000 men, of which a mere 12,000 could be spared from garrison duties to be put into the field. But for the French to gain the heart of Holland, an attack from the sea was necessary. This was rendered impossible by Admiral Michel de Ruyter's victory over the English and French fleets at Southwold Bay on June 7.

The French land forces, therefore, detoured, and on June 12 crossed the Rhine in order to attack Amsterdam and The Hague from the east. The crossing of that "natural" boundary, which met with little opposition, was the high point of Louis XIV's military career and was flamboyantly celebrated as such. Louis himself took part in that grand strategic maneuver and for once proved himself a better and more prudent director of the operation than the more experienced but impetuous Condé.

The triumph came to nothing, however, for the divided command—Louis and Louvois from behind the lines arguing with Turenne, who was arguing with Condé—gave the Dutch time to flood the country between their capitals and the French army by opening the dikes.

The Dutch offered to make peace, but rejected Louis's terms as too harsh. A coup d'état in the Dutch government put William of Orange into power on July 3, 1672, thus unifying the nation which had been divided between patriotically and financially oriented parties. William dedicated himself to saving his country from annihilation.

After de Ruyter's naval victory at Zeeland in June, 1673, which prevented the English from landing troops to reinforce the French, the Dutch again rejected Louis XIV's peace terms. Louis was therefore obliged to withdraw some of his forces from Holland. The unlucky year for the French ended (actually in early 1674) with the English Parliament forcing Charles II to withdraw from the war.

This action by England's Protestant Parliament was largely the result of Louis's having furthered his diplomacy by arranging the marriage of the childless Charles II's brother James, a pro-Catholic who would probably be the next king of England, to a Catholic princess, Mary Beatrice of Modena (Italy), a great-niece of Cardinal Mazarin. That maneuver made it clear to the English Parliament that Louis was aiming to Catholicize England and bring it into the hegemony of Catholic nations on the Continent.

By that time the Dutch had organized new resistance and gained allies, amongst whom was Spain. It was against these powers that Louis XIV moved next.

The opening of that second front resulted in another swift conquest by the French of Spanish Franche-Comté and also in the invasion of the southern part of Holland. Turenne also invaded the Black Forest region of Holland's German allies, but lost his life on the expedition. The death of Turenne was a crushing blow for the French. It was followed by another, the retirement of the elderly Condé, who was in poor health.

The war then entered a long phase which brought the proud Louis XIV face to face with the reality that what he had thought would be a swift and decisive humiliation of Holland was actually a humiliating stalemate for him.

Louis's great blunder had been his insistence on impossible conditions for peace in 1672 and 1673. These included a demand that the Dutch send a mission every year to Versailles with the gift of a gold medal commemorating Louis's generosity in granting them peace at all. By 1676, Louis was brush-

Louis II de Bourbon, Duc de Condé ("the Great Condé") (1621–86), by Antoine Coysevox.

ing aside the praise and flattery lavished on him for the few French successes—in Sicily and the Caribbean against Spain, which was allied with Holland—and almost apologizing for the war's lasting so long.

The year 1677, however, opened with a surprise offensive in Flanders, disguised by brilliant court fetes at Versailles that led the enemies of France to think the French had no intention of taking the field until winter was over. The summer campaign brought France several splendid victories, to which William of Orange could reply only with diplomacy; he married the English king's niece Mary, James Stuart's daughter by his first wife who was a Protestant. The marriage contract provided for a permanent Anglo-Dutch Protestant alliance, quite upsetting the 1670 Treaty of Dover which had been so favorable to Louis XIV.

The long war had put an unendurable strain on France, where the people of several regions were so close to starvation that they started armed revolts against the militaristic government. Devout Frenchmen believed that the wretched state of their country was God's judgment on their king's flagrant extramarital affair with the beautiful, intelligent, hot-tempered Françoise Athénaïs de Montespan—a double adultery, since she, too, was married. Louis figured that he had better make peace on the best terms he could get. He was sure that he could get good ones, for Lionne and Pomponne had built up a diplomatic corps of unbelievably shrewd efficiency.

A peace conference at Nijmegen (also spelled Nymwegen and, in French, Nimégues) in Holland resulted in several treaties. The principal one—between Louis and the Dutch—was signed on August 11, 1678. Thanks to England's mediation of the conference, Holland came off much better than might have been expected. The war, however, had severely damaged the finances of the Dutch and their trade. Spain had to pay the greater part of the bill.

The result of the various cessions of important territory to France was that Louis XIV acquired abroad the name of "the terror of Europe." At home, however, the exuberant French officially entitled him Louis the Great, a title he kept the rest of his life. The Sun King had reached the high noon of his *gloire*, and France reached a height of world power it had not achieved since the reign of Charlemagne some eight hundred years earlier.

In spite of these outward triumphs, Louis XIV was inwardly becoming a chastened and somewhat subdued man. The eloquent and powerful preaching of the Jansenist (that is, to put it briefly, Puritanical Catholic) divine Jacques Bossuet had begun to convince him that he should reform his scandalous private life—if, indeed, anything about Louis XIV's life was private. The fiery Mme de Montespan's temper tantrums had begun to weary him anyway, and she had become repulsively fat. Louis tardily returned some of his queen's affection for him.

Another influence on Louis XIV's reformation, and the greatest influence on his life after the death of Mazarin in 1661 and of Anne of Austria in 1666, was Françoise d'Aubigné Scarron, the Marquise de Maintenon.

The daughter of an impoverished family of illustrious antecedents, Françoise had had a miserable childhood and was saved from the isolated life of a convent only by marrying, at the age of sixteen, the comic poet and novelist Paul Scarron. Scarron was forty-two years old at the time of this Platonic marriage and had been a sadly deformed cripple for twelve years. The couple lived in poverty, but attracted a circle of intellectuals in Paris who admired Scarron's wit and his wife's charm and intelligence. Among those friends was Mme de Montespan, who became Françoise Scarron's devoted friend—probably because the two women were equal in intelligence but so different in personality that they complemented each other.

Mme de Montespan, who was of an ancient, rich, noble family and married to a rich nobleman, did not forget her old friend after Scarron's death in 1660 left his widow in extreme poverty. After Mme de Montespan began presenting Louis XIV with children—seven, of whom only four survived childhood—she entrusted them to Françoise Scarron, who, childless herself, loved and cared for them devotedly.

Louis XIV often visited these children at the house he had provided for them and their foster-mother at the present Number 25, Boulevard des Invalides, Paris. Although Louis was envious of his son by Maria Theresa and treated him cruelly, he liked children in general. He was particularly fond of the eldest of Mme de Montespan's and his brood, Louis Auguste, the future Duc du Maine. Louis XIV did not, however, like Françoise Scarron very much at that time. He thought her a tedious moralizer, and too plebeian in her tastes for his grandiose way of life.

Françoise Scarron fought off the doctors—like all others at that time, they killed more often than they cured—who were trying to remedy Louis Auguste's semiparalyzed leg. She herself saw to it that the child surmounted that birth injury with only a slight limp. Such patient care made Louis XIV look differently at the governess. He rewarded her for all her services with the château of Maintenon, near Chartres, which gave her the right to the title by which she is best known to history—Mme de Maintenon. And Louis discovered that in her pleasant if unexciting company he could find the peace that

Mme de Montespan's rages made impossible. With Mme de Maintenon he could also have instructive conversations, which Maria Theresa's stupidity prevented.

Presently the gossipy courtiers were calling Mme de Maintenon "Mme de Maintenant" (meaning "now"—or "the present favorite"). Naturally this change in the king's affections— he had given Mme de Maintenon a suite in the palace of Versailles near his own apartments—destroyed the friendship Mme de Montespan had once showed her. They became deadly enemies.

Mme de Montespan played her cards badly. The triumph of the governess was marked when, in the hearing of plenty of courtiers, Mme de Maintenon remarked to her rival as they met on the staircase leading to the king's apartments: "You are going down, Madame? I am going up."

Up she went indeed, but not to the king's bedroom. There seems to have been no romantic attachment between Louis and Françoise at that time. Mme de Maintenon's motives appear to have been relatively unselfish—a rarity in a court that thrived on intrigue and self-interest. She seems to have had most at heart the improvement of the king's morals, the elevation of his spiritual side, and, through those aims, the welfare of her country.

Before Mme de Maintenon died, she destroyed all her intimate papers, saying that she wished to be an enigma to historians. Her wish was granted. We know from her acts that she was altruistic, deeply religious, and something of a prude; also, that she was too insecure to be loyal to friends whose behavior and opinions threatened her relations with the king, that perhaps she was a bigot, that she was hypocritical. The great mystery is the precise nature of the power she held over Louis, three years younger than she, who was the most powerful ruler in the world and knew that he was.

Françoise d'Aubigné Scarron, Marquise de Maintenon (1635–1719), second wife of Louis XIV, by Pierre Mignard.

The change in Louis XIV's attitudes was quickly reflected in the court life. The king declared himself against the flagrant vice in which he felt the young courtiers, even those of his own blood, were indulging. He insisted that everyone consider going to mass his first obligation, and that behavior in church be reverent and decorous. There were just as many court entertainments as ever, and as much gambling, but the repressive atmosphere created by the reformed monarch chilled the former gaiety of court life. The court, as one commentator said, "sweated hypocrisy." Boredom replaced spontaneity. More and more often the courtiers sneaked away from Versailles for visits to the livelier diversions that Paris offered.

The king's conversion was actually superficial also. Apparently he believed that the mere abandoning of "sin" automatically made him a virtuous Christian. It was impossible for him to subject himself to the self-criticism that might have made him truly repentant and turned him toward obedience to higher laws than his own. Christ's commandment of love, His emphasis on humility, His care for the poor, were actually repulsive to Louis XIV, who disliked having to listen to those passages in the Gospels and the Epistles that expounded them. He hated to hear of the wretched plight of most of his subjects and turned a deaf ear to the pleas of, say, Louis Bourdaloue for prison reform, and a blind eye to the labors of Saint Vincent de Paul's missionaries on behalf of the poor, the sick, the galley slaves, and Christians who had been captured by Muslims.

Louis XIV's remoteness from actual conditions in his realm is symbolized by his making Versailles the capital of his kingdom on May 6, 1682. The seat of the government of the king of France was thereafter to be as distant from his subjects as the government of the earth is said to be from the mortals who inhabit it.

The king's notion of divine help and guidance was that God was in his debt because Louis had done so much for Him. Now that Louis had reached the summit of his *gloire*, he seems to have reasoned that the change in his morals would persuade God to repay him in full and with interest. No blessing henceforth could possibly be denied him.

Louis XIV's disregard for the comfort of others inflicted on the ailing Maria Theresa a two-month's journey of inspection to the army and the fortresses on France's eastern frontier. When the queen returned to Versailles she took to her bed exhausted, and suffering from a boil in her armpit. The inefficient ministrations of the king's doctor, Guy Crescent Fagon, greatly hastened her end. On July 30, 1683, after an illness of three days, she died in the arms of Mme de Maintenon, whom she adored for having, as she said, "given my husband back to me."

Louis XIV was deeply affected by the death of his wife. "Poor woman," he said, "this is the only time she has caused me any grief." Her sister-in-law wrote: "It is not an exaggeration to say that all France's happiness has died with her."

The king's despondency was short-lived. Probably on October 9, 1683, he married Françoise de Maintenon. The ceremony was so secret that the exact date, and even its existence, have never been ascertained and can only be—fairly reliably—guessed at. A year later, Louis XIV turned Mme de Montespan out of her apartment, which was next to his.*

---

* Mme de Montespan, however, did not leave the court itself until 1691, when she retired to a convent. Her death, in 1707, occurred when Louis XIV was so involved with the War of the Spanish Succession that he scarcely noticed it. Mme de Maintenon was the only person at court who shed a tear.

VII

DESCENT
FROM THE PINNACLE

Louis XIV's health began to fail about the time of his second marriage. Dizzy spells, colds that brought on temporary deafness, and attacks of malaria, rheumatism, and gout made him miserable. He swallowed quantities of pills and purges, was given innumerable emetics and enemas, and was frequently bled. Becoming something of a hypochondriac, he greatly enjoyed having read to him the accounts of his illnesses and treatments as published by his doctors in the court bulletin. In 1684, he had all his teeth pulled and also underwent the first of two excruciatingly painful operations, performed, of course, without any anesthetic. (The second was in 1686.)

Somehow he survived all these ailments and the remedies prescribed for them by the sadistic Dr. Fagon. Without Fagon, Louis might have lived to be ninety instead of only seventy-seven, for he had an iron constitution.

The king's enemies and the superstitious regarded his physical sufferings as divine punishments for his moral lapses. Probably Louis also took this view, for he was too uncritical of himself to perceive that his illnesses were largely the result of overindulgence at the table and too great a fondness for the cold, damp air of Versailles. He became much concerned with the state of his soul and submerged himself in the shallow pool of his unimaginative religious convictions. He had always disliked arguments and novelty; now he began to equate order with orthodoxy.

Hence, Louis XIV seems to have interpreted the frequent recommendations of his advisers that he get rid of the Protestant minority in his kingdom—about one million of the total twenty million inhabitants—as a means by which he would ensure salvation for his soul.

The advisers in question were principally churchmen, who definitely urged the obliteration of heresy. The reformed Louis was now listening to clerics' opinions about political matters. In addition, the bureaucrats whom Louis himself had empowered maintained that an orderly unity of government was impossible when there was more than one religion in France. Religion in the seventeenth century had the same binding force on a community that nationalism often has today.

The last fifty years of the sixteenth century were a period of almost continual warfare between French Protestants (Huguenots) and French Catholics. Indeed, all of western Europe had then been engaged in conflicts motivated as much by religious arguments as by territorial and economic interests. The issue then was toleration of the new Protestantism. The political question was whether Protestants, almost always a minority of a population, could be loyal citizens when they rejected the religion of the state. Such rejection must mean refusal to acknowledge the government, for church and state were one.

Of course, each side—Protestant and Catholic—maintained that the other was utterly wrong about religion and fought to convert its opponents to a belief that would save their soul for sure. The Catholics maintained that only confession and absolution—the mediation of the Church—could redeem a soul. The Protestants argued that forgiveness of sin and the imposition of penance by a state-appointed priest subjected a man's soul to the judgment of the state's human agents. These state-appointed priests, the Protestants said, were less capable of awarding salvation than God himself. But this fine point of theology mattered less to a ruler and his ministers than the danger they saw in permitting a subversive element to survive. For by denying the efficacy of the state church to grant salvation, the Protestants were also denying the total authority of the state.

Every one of the countries involved in the great and bloody dispute had to solve the problem in order to have any kind of peace either within or outside its boundaries. In France, the solution was the Edict of Nantes, issued by Henry IV on April 13, 1598.

That document stated that although the established religion of France was Catholicism, the Huguenots might legally worship in the churches ("temples") that they had built previous to 1597. Huguenots could hold government offices and could bring legal cases before special courts—that is, ones where they would not be compelled to swear loyalty to institutions that offended their beliefs. They were also allowed to keep the cities they had fortified while fighting against the Catholics. The Edict of Nantes was the first official act of religious toleration in Christian history.

Under Louis XIII, however, Cardinal Richelieu determined to eradicate the Huguenots on the ground that they were undermining the unity of government he was trying to establish. Rather accurately defining their existence as a "republic within the kingdom," he made war on them from 1624 to 1628, when he captured their principal fortress of La Rochelle. The subsequent Peace of Alais, in 1629, deprived the

Louis XIV about 1683, by François Girardon.

Huguenots of all their other strongholds, but permitted them freedom of worship. Without their fortifications, the Huguenots, it was thought, would cause little trouble.

Cardinal Mazarin took a much more lenient attitude and even gave an important government post to a Huguenot. During Mazarin's regime, there were only petty, localized disturbances of a religious nature, and the Huguenots took no part in the wars of the Fronde, which were largely directed against the cardinal. Protestant leadership was, by Mazarin's death, no longer in the hands of the nobles who could raise troops by dint of their ancient feudal rights and privileges.

Colbert greatly favored the Huguenots, for they were an essential part of the labor force he needed for the success of his planned economy. The Huguenots believed that the rewards of hard work were an indication of God's favor and so tended to be more industrious than Catholics. As the Huguenots thrived financially, they agitated less.

The Huguenots were principally skilled artisans, but there were also among them many in the medical profession, and many others were engaged in trade. Their industry and frugality made them prosperous, and so they excited the envy of their less successful competitors, especially when those were Catholics. The Catholics also thought the Huguenots old-fashioned, dull, and prudish, and regarded their piety as a kind of conscious reproach to orthodox forms of worship.

Louis XIV, who understood practically nothing of the Huguenots' way of thinking or way of life, accepted those clichés of judgment. His Jesuit confessor, Père François de La Chaise (for whom Paris's most famous cemetery is named), and other Jesuits did not disabuse the king's mind of such shallow opinions. The Jesuits of that period were sworn to combat and destroy heresy by any means whatever.

The greatest instigators of Louis's hatred of the Huguenots, however, appear to have been Le Tellier, now chancellor of France, and Louvois, Louis XIV's highly efficient war minister. Father and son had long desired Colbert's downfall because he opposed their warmongering as a drain on the treasury. They saw that by encouraging the king to persecute the finance minister's protégés, the Huguenots, they might put an end to their rival's influence on the sovereign. They convinced Louis that the Huguenots' beliefs made those worthy citizens literal traitors to him.

That conviction was all Louis XIV needed to acquiesce in the measures that the Assembly of Clergy had already forced into execution in spite of the king's public announcement that he would abide by the terms of the Edict of Nantes. The clergy had subtly blocked that policy by acknowledging the edict as a law and at the same time insisting that any right it did not specifically grant the Huguenots was illegal. Since the edict did not spell out, for example, that a Huguenot might be a tailor or a teacher or a midwife, the clergy maintained that no Protestant could, therefore, legally practice such an occupation. Corrupt judges, looking out for their own interests, did not hesitate to hand down decisions that would follow the new trend of official thinking but which were ruinous to the Protestants. From 1665 onward, the Huguenots were more and more victimized by this cynical "legislation."

That persecution was combined, in 1676, with bribery. Protestants who would renounce their faith and could produce a certificate of conversion to Catholicism were rewarded with a liberal cash payment. The conversion did not even have to be sincere; regular attendance at mass and no loose skeptical talk were sufficient to satisfy the authorities that the acceptance of orthodoxy was genuine. The system succeeded to an astonishing degree. After all, if the great Huguenot leader Henri IV had accepted Catholicism in order to get control of Paris ("Paris is worth a mass") and thereby win the throne, why should a later Huguenot suffer injustice when he could be paid to become free of it?

Many Huguenots, however, were too steadfast in their belief to stoop to such indignity. These, who were usually the richer and the more farsighted Protestants, left France for countries where their religious conviction would be respected and protected. And after the offensive decree of June 17, 1681, that all Protestant children must renounce their religion for Catholicism at the age of seven, England, Denmark, and Holland actually invited the Huguenots to refuge, promising them a livelihood in their new abodes. Thus about 200,000 useful French citizens left their native land.

The Sun King's council then perceived that such emigration was ruining French industry and trade, not to mention depriving the new French navy of sailors. Alarmed at the thought that his war machine might be irreparably damaged by loss of revenue and military personnel—for the Huguenots made good and willing soldiers as well as sailors—Louis XIV signed an order forbidding any Huguenot to leave France on pain of being sentenced to the galleys for life. Life was shockingly brief after such a sentence was carried out; in fact, most victims died of maltreatment on their way to the southern ports where the galleys were harbored.

The next thing to be done was to step up the conversions of the now captive Huguenots. (Plenty of them, however, still managed to slip across the long and none-too-well-patrolled frontiers in spite of the rewards offered to anyone who caught them.) Soldiers were quartered in the homes of recalcitrant Protestants and were given full liberty to use any means they wished to effect conversion of the household. Soldiers being what they were then, these means were brut-

ally persuasive. This fiendish measure of repression, known as
the *dragonnade* (from "dragoon"—a soldier), produced 38,000
conversions within a year from its inception in March, 1681.
It also produced such violent protests from all the Protestant
nations of Europe that Louis eventually had to modify it in
order to safeguard his foreign policy.

In the meantime, the *dragonnade*'s reign of terror continued. So did the stubbornness of devout Huguenots. As
Voltaire remarked in his history of Louis XIV's reign: "It is
known only too well that the greater the sufferings men en-
dure for their religion, the more they cling to it." If the
Catholics could pay for conversions, the rich Protestants could
also pay to prevent them. And by 1682, the bold Huguenots
took up arms in some regions of France, only to have their
revolt immediately quashed and its leaders horribly tortured.

Louvois kept much information about this unrest from
the king. Instead, the war minister stressed the number of
conversions produced by the implacable *dragonnade* he
directed. Indeed Louis began to believe that God had appointed him to be His agent in restoring to His Church all
who had been tempted away from it. The king also began to
believe that there were so few unconverted Huguenots left in
his kingdom that the Edict of Nantes was a useless piece of
legislation. Furthermore, Louis recognized that so long as
the edict remained in effect, Protestant pastors could continue ministering to the faithful and even reconverting the
new Catholics. Lastly, if Louis repealed the edict, thus making
Protestantism again illegal in France, he could prove his devotion to Pope Innocent XI, who was then at odds with him.
Thus he could demonstrate that he was the leader of the
Catholic party in Europe—a title that would fully complete his
gloire, which had reached new heights with his acquisition in

1681 of the powerful city of Strasbourg,* and of Luxembourg in 1684, after a brief and destructive campaign.

The court had gone to Fontainebleau for the autumn hunting. There, on October 18, 1685, Louis XIV revoked the Edict of Nantes. The document that accomplished the revocation, the Edict of Fontainebleau, had been prepared by the aged Chancellor Le Tellier, who regarded it as the crowning achievement of his long career as a public servant. Signed by Louis XIV, it stated that "the best and largest part of our subjects of the so-called reformed religion have embraced Catholicism, and now, since the execution of the Edict of Nantes remains useless, we have judged that we can do nothing better to wipe out the memory of the troubles, of the confusion, of the evils that the progress of that false religion has caused in our kingdom . . . than to revoke entirely the said Edict."

The Edict of Fontainebleau ordered the destruction of all remaining Protestant "temples," the exile of all Protestant ministers, the end of all Protestant religious services, the closing of Protestant schools, and the baptism in the Catholic faith of all infants born to Protestants. No Protestant layman was to leave France.

The edict was enforced with great brutality. The *dragonnade* doubled and redoubled its intensity. Men were tortured. Women were stripped naked and whipped. Protestants caught trying to flee the country or worshiping in secret were

---

* Strasbourg, the principal city of Alsace, was practically a free and independent city in a region that was predominantly German. Louis XIV acquired this rich, strategically located, well-fortified stronghold on September 20, 1681, through bribery and threats. Until the Treaty of Versailles in 1919 awarded it to France, possession of Strasbourg was hotly contended by France and Germany, and the whole region of Alsace changed hands several times. Today both French and German are spoken in Strasbourg, and the customs of its people are an amusing mixture of the two cultures.

sent to the galleys or deported to the American colonies. Protestant pastors who stubbornly remained in France after the two weeks given them to leave were hanged. Converts who only pretended to take Communion were burned alive. The bodies of those who had refused the last rites of the Catholic church were flung on manure piles to rot. But pockets of resistance remained in spite of much missionary work on the part of the Catholic church, and these were a chronic irritation until the end of Louis XIV's reign.

The response of French Catholics to the revocation of the Edict of Nantes was wildly enthusiastic. A few skeptics, notably Vauban and Saint-Simon, lamented the waste and the immorality of the decree, but Louis's prestige among the majority of his subjects reached a new peak.

Such was not the reaction abroad. Even Pope Innocent XI, whom Louis had hoped to conciliate by his defense of the faith, regarded the Edict of Fontainebleau as a piece of folly. Louis, the pope said, "looked more to the advantages of his realm than to the kingdom of God." The elector of Brandenburg, who was laying the foundations for the kingdom of Prussia, welcomed fugitive Huguenots to his developing country, as did the governments of Holland and Switzerland.

By 1689, Vauban would lament that the enemies of France acquired from the Protestant emigration, which the French could not stop, "eight or nine thousand sailors, five or six hundred army officers, ten to twelve thousand veteran soldiers." Not to mention, for example, the sixty thousand clothworkers who found asylum in England and greatly benefited the industry of that nation, which was soon to be in arms against France. Conversely, French industry and commerce suffered irreparable damage, and much money went out of the country.

The only defense possible for this egregious blunder of Louis XIV's, which was to bring moral and political bankruptcy on his country, is that he acted according to the nature of his times. Religious tolerance was an idea not unknown, but Holland was the only nation that had even begun to practice it. The Protestant countries had persecuted Catholics as much as Louis XIV was hounding the Huguenots. The blame rests ultimately on Louis himself for believing, as it were, his own publicity, and not questioning the reports or suspecting the motives of Louvois and the Jesuits, and for removing himself out of earshot from the voice of his people.

The Huguenot exiles stirred up great hostility to France in the countries where they found refuge and hospitality. This propaganda had the greatest success in England.

England's Protestant King Charles II had kept a neat balance between his royal prerogative and the rights of Parliament, and an equally nice balance between the money he took from Louis XIV for favoring French aims and the true political interests of his own kingdom. The death of Charles II, on February 6, 1685, left the English throne to his brother James, an ardent Roman Catholic. The revocation of the Edict of Nantes and the tales of persecution told by the refugee Huguenots made the English dread the not unlikely possibility that their new king, James II, would reestablish Catholicism as the state religion in England and visit on English Protestants the same horrors that his cousin Louis XIV had perpetrated on the Huguenots.

Louis encouraged James to be an absolute monarch, and the Jesuits urged him to restore the power of the Catholic church. James was more than willing to do both, but he was a poor politician and he had no sense of timing. His humorless attempts to achieve his desires were so repugnant to the English, and so contrary to English tradition, that on June 30, 1688, a large group of the Whig party (Protestants and Parliamentarians) secretly invited the Protestant William of Orange to take the throne of England, from which they would help him push his father-in-law.

William, who was to the Protestants what Louis XIV was to the Catholics, landed in England with 14,000 soldiers of various nationalities on November 5, 1688. Most of James II's army deserted to William, who had a reasonably good claim to the throne in his own right (he was a grandson of King Charles I), plus the better claim of his Protestant wife Mary. The fact that James II had had a son,* born on June 10, 1688, who could inherit the crown, made the Protestant English all the more determined to turn the throne over to the Protestant succession.

James II fled, but was captured. Later Parliament allowed him to escape to France through a door in his prison-castle that was deliberately left open.

William of Orange was proclaimed King William III of England on February 13, 1689. His wife was made joint sovereign with him as Queen Mary II. The succession to this childless couple was settled on Mary's Protestant sister Anne Stuart, who became Queen Anne in 1702. The Catholic branch of the Stuart family was therefore declared by Parliament ineligible for rule in England.

That sequence of events, known in England as the "Glorious" or "Bloodless Revolution," was to cause almost a century of bloodshed elsewhere by involving most of Europe in a second Hundred Years War.

The principal cause of that long and bloody conflict was the continued aggression of Louis XIV on states bordering

---

* James Francis Edward Stuart, later to be known as the "Old Pretender." His eldest son, Charles Edward Stuart, was known as the "Young Pretender"—and, to his supporters, as the "Young Chevalier" and "Bonnie Prince Charlie." Both were Catholics, and both made unsuccessful invasions of England in an attempt to get the throne to which they "pretended" they had a legal right.

the Rhine. He had never lost sight of his objective to extend France's boundaries to that river. After the Treaty of Nijmegen, Louis had pursued his aim by skillful diplomacy backed up by his mighty army.

The triumph of that forceful diplomacy was the Peace of Ratisbon, concluded in August, 1684. This twenty-year truce confirmed French possession of the territories on France's eastern frontier that Louis had annexed. Emperor Leopold I of Austria was too involved with driving the Turks out of his eastern lands to protest Louis's encroachments on principalities along the Rhine that owed allegiance to the Empire and so deserved aid from the emperor. Spain was too weak to defend its strategic towns in Flanders and Franche-Comté.

The truce agreed upon at Ratisbon, however, satisfied none of the states that had made concessions. They were alarmed by Louis's stretching the terms of the peace—he claimed, for example, the Rhenish Palatinate in the name of his sister-in-law, the daughter of its recently deceased elector— and they were roused by expressions of nationalistic (i.e., anti-French) spirit in their realms as well as by Louis XIV's abuse of the Huguenots. Under the instigation of William of Orange they* formed the League of Augsburg on July 9, 1686, for the purpose of maintaining the terms of the Peace of Westphalia, the Treaty of Nijmegen, and the Peace of Ratisbon.

Instead of being the leader of Catholic Europe, as Louis XIV thought he had become by the revocation of the Edict of Nantes, he now found both Catholic and Protestant states allied against him. The pope put his moral weight behind the league and encouraged the emperor to make war on France as the only way to stop Louis XIV's aggression. Louis's old

* The contracting parties were Emperor Leopold I, the kings of Spain and of Sweden, and the rulers of several German principalities.

dread of a coalition against him was now increased by his fear of being encircled.

Under pressure from Louvois, Louis XIV had dismissed the moderate Pomponne as his foreign minister. As Pomponne's successor, Louis appointed Colbert de Croissy, an ill-tempered little man who worked closely with Louvois on a more adventurous foreign policy of aggressive confrontation. These advisers were too intent on their own schemes to see the general trend of European politics. Louis trusted them because he was too egocentric to understand or wish to understand a broad diplomatic point of view. Their provincial ignorance of English political thinking led them to induce Louis to back the "wrong horse" (James II) in England. They also advised him that Emperor Leopold could not dislodge the Turks from his eastern domains—as the emperor succeeded in doing by September 6, 1688. Louis XIV had refused Leopold aid against the Turks.

Louis thus had to face two formidable opponents. William III had consecrated himself to destroying the power of France. "I will burn Versailles," he declared, "or perish in the attempt." Freed from the menace of the Turks, Leopold I could now defend his western territories and match his Hapsburg ambitions with Louis XIV's Bourbon ones. Whereas, for once, Louis had not wanted war, he now found that war was inevitable.

The only way out of the political trap into which Louis had allowed his ministers to lead him was to mount a lightning-fast attack on the hostile states that had almost ringed France. Under the legal fiction of asserting the claims of his sister-in-law to the Rhenish Palatinate, Louis issued an ultimatum to the emperor on September 24, 1688, that he would occupy the Rhineland for three months until the claim was settled—naturally, in his favor.

The declaration was really a declaration of war, and the occupation was actually a blitzkrieg. Once the French had captured the key fortress of Philippsburg on the east bank of the Rhine, on October 30, 1688, they proceeded to devastate the entire region. By June 1, 1689, its four principal cities had been burned, as well as about fifty castles and countless villages, along with all the crops whether in the fields or in barns. This horrible devastation—a scorched-earth policy—made the area incapable of supporting an army. Thus Louis's new acquisitions in Alsace, on the opposite (west) bank of the Rhine, were relatively safe from recapture. In this military sense, the ravaging of the palatinate was good strategy. In the broad political sense, it was a fatal error, for it inflamed German resistance and led to an even greater coalition and encirclement than had previously menaced France. Indeed, the destruction caused the Franco-German antipathy that lasted until the end of World War II.

By September, 1689, William III had declared war on France and had brought England and the United Provinces into an alliance with Emperor Leopold I. Their states joined those already in the League of Augsburg, and the now huge coalition became the Grand Alliance, dedicated to accomplishing the aims of the league. The war is generally known as the War of the League of Augsburg. (Its American phase was known as King William's War.) In 1690, Savoy joined the alliance, and Sweden lent it aid.

France was now completely surrounded by hostile nations and had not a single ally. The balance of power in Europe had utterly shifted. Louis XIV was at the turning point of his career.

Louvois determined to fight a defensive war. The French had a navy of one hundred men-of-war and 25,000 seamen. The army numbered 300,000 men and was in excellent training, though the cavalry suffered from France's inability to breed and supply good horses. Three French armies took the field: a defensive force in Alsace, under Marshal de Lorges; one against the duke of Savoy, under Lieutenant General Catinat; and one in Flanders, under the Duc de Luxembourg, the able successor of Turenne and Condé. The fleet was under the nominal command of Louis XIV's ten-year-old son by Mme de Montespan, but was well directed by Admiral de Tourville, who defeated the Anglo-Dutch navy off Beachy Head on July 1, 1690.

On the same day occurred in Ireland the only engagement of the war still remembered except by specialists, and the only one to have far-reaching political results. The dethroned James II and his family had arrived in France in January, 1689. Louis XIV had welcomed them with lavish gifts and installed them in luxury in the palace of Saint-Germain, where the ill-fated former monarch of England held a petty court. Like any other exile, James immediately started measures of revenge.

Both to aid his humiliated cousin and to distract William III from military activity on the Continent, Louis XIV sent James with an army to Ireland. Louis counted on the Irish Catholics to support James against their new and unpopular Protestant sovereign. William moved against these ill-armed and ill-commanded forces and defeated them decisively at the Boyne River. Ever since, William's color orange has been to good Catholic Irishmen like red to a bull, and a favorable mention of "Boyne water" an invitation to a brawl.

The French, nevertheless, seemed invincible on the Continent and prepared to invade England. The naval battle of La Hogue, on May 29, 1692, however, restored control of the English Channel to England and reduced the French fleet to commerce-destroying operations.

In 1693, Louis XIV reached a climax of military success

on land with Luxembourg's victory over the allies at Neer-winden on July 19. After that battle, Louis himself withdrew from the field and never thereafter followed his army in person. That same year, Catinat again defeated the duke of Savoy, and de Tourville captured a treasure-laden Anglo-Dutch convoy.

Louis's retirement from the front to Versailles did not mean that he ceased to direct his armies. Rather, he exercised more and more control over them. Louvois had died on July 16, 1691, and Louis did not fully trust Louvois's twenty-two-year-old son and successor, the Marquis de Barbézieux, as war minister, or his other youthful advisers. The burden of conducting the war now fell almost wholly on Louis's shoulders.

Not being a professional soldier, Louis concerned himself with gaining temporary advantages and sacrificed long-term gains to them. As a result, French strategy grew ineffective; its aims were divided, and victories were not well followed up. The war slogged along, exhausting both sides more with boredom than with bloodshed.

William III, who rarely won a battle but never lost a war, took advantage of this lull to reorganize the alliance's forces and to recoup some of the allies' losses. On January 4, 1695, the Duc de Luxembourg died, and William was able to recapture the key fortress of Namur. Louis was so angry at that loss, for which one of his illegitimate sons was responsible, that he took out his rage by breaking his walking stick on the back of a servant whom he caught filching a biscuit. He told his confessor that he did not think that unjust explosion of temper an offense in God's sight.

In June of the following year (1696), Louis's diplomacy won the duke of Savoy over to the French side. Money had greased the wheels of the secret negotiations, and so had the promise of Louis's grandson as a husband for the duke's

François de Salignac de la Mothe-Fénelon (1651–1715), by Vivien.

daughter. The maneuver forced Emperor Leopold to abandon the Italian frontier and agree to the neutralization of Italy. The Imperial forces were thereafter no great danger to Louis XIV—and no great help to William III.

William, therefore, had to direct the alliance virtually single-handed. A cousin of Louis XIV, he was as different in character from the Sun King as he was dedicated to crushing him. Cold and severe in temperament, physically frail, neurotic, and solemn, he hated amusements and any kind of gaiety. Ironically, William was a product of French civilization, an example of how, under Louis XIV's inspiration, it had spread even to hostile lands. William spoke, wrote, and thought in French; he never learned English, and he was far more at ease with Frenchmen than with his English subjects.

Shocked by the desertion of Savoy, faced with a financial crisis in England, and dismayed by the Indian raids which Louis's recently reinstated governor of Canada, Comte de Frontenac, was launching on English settlements in America, William was ready to discuss peace. In addition, he feared a new offensive in Flanders from the French, whose army was now reinforced with Savoyard troops.

Louis XIV was equally ready. The terrible winter of 1694–95, which extended freezing temperatures into May, made crops scanty and added famine to the hardships of the French people, who had already been taxed to the point of destitution to pay for the war. Even so, France's finances were near collapse. Internal trade was ruined because the war drained the manpower that might have kept roads and bridges in repair. The enemy fleet had seriously damaged shipping and fishing, bankrupting coastal towns which also had to support troops quartered upon them. The population declined by about four million.

At this time, Bishop François de La Mothe-Fénelon, tutor of Louis XIV's grandson, addressed a daring letter to the king:

> For some thirty years past your chief ministers have overturned all the ancient maxims of state to raise your authority to the utmost, because it was in their hands. No one spoke any more of the state and its laws; they spoke only of the king and his good pleasure. They have extended your revenues and your expenditure without limit. They have raised you to the skies in order, they say, to efface the grandeur of all your predecessors combined, but actually they have improverished all France to establish at the court a monstrous and incurable luxury. They have wished to elevate you upon the ruin of every class in the

state—as if you could be great while ruining all the subjects upon whom your greatness depends. . . . They have made your name hateful—and the whole French nation unbearable—to neighboring peoples. . . . You have always wished to dictate peace, to impose conditions, instead of arranging them with moderation; that is why no peace has endured. Your enemies, shamefully struck down, have only one thought: to stand up again and unite themselves against you. Is it surprising? You have not even stayed within the limits of the peace terms that you so proudly dictated. In time of peace you have made war and immense conquests. . . . Such conduct has aroused and united all Europe against you.

Meanwhile your people, whom you should have loved as your children, and who have till now been devoted to you, are dying of hunger. The cultivation of the earth is almost abandoned; the towns and the countryside are depopulated; all industry languishes, and no longer supports the workers. All commerce is destroyed.

You have consumed half the wealth and vitality of the nation to make and defend vain conquests abroad. . . . All France is now but a vast hospital, desolate and without provisions. . . . You must humble yourself under the powerful hand of God, if you do not wish Him to humble you. . . . You must ask for peace, and expiate by that humiliation all the glory which you have made your idol. . . .

Louis XIV never saw that letter. Mme de Maintenon, to whom it was sent for delivery to him, did not dare read it to the king. She knew that Louis would only produce pragmatic answers to Fénelon's theoretical morality. Nevertheless, the letter expressed the spirit of the French during those troublous times.

Louis XIV was not wholly unaware, however, of what Fénelon was calling to his attention. Certainly he knew that four armies were at his frontiers, that his fleet was impotent, that his people were restless. It is perhaps much to his credit that he did not surrender. His pride would never have permitted that betrayal of his ambitions, but he did recognize that the pride of France was greater than his personal *gloire*. At the end of 1696, he sent secret agents to inform William III that he was ready to yield all the territories, except Strasbourg, that he had annexed since the Treaty of Nijmegen.

William III, however, demanded that Louis XIV recognize him as legal king of England before any peace conference could begin. Louis still maintained that James II was England's rightful ruler. And James was continually plotting another expedition from Saint-Germain against William, or a scheme to assassinate the alleged usurper.

After the death of Colbert de Croissy in 1696, Pomponne had returned to power as Louis XIV's foreign minister. True to his former character, he was moderate in his negotiations, having never been much in favor of territorial expansion. He induced William to temper his demands. Two years of conferences began.

The peace treaty finally signed at Ryswick on September 20, 1697, was a personal triumph for William III. Louis XIV was compelled to recognize him as England's legitimate ruler. William had defeated Louis's predatory designs on the east bank of the Rhine; had safeguarded the Dutch, whom Louis had wished to destroy; and had made Louis change the tone of his policy.

It was thought, too, that William III had restored the balance of power in Europe by humbling Louis XIV. Louis, however, had his eye on bigger gains than a few strongholds in Flanders.

VIII

AN END TO GLORY

After the War of the League of Augsburg had proved to Louis XIV the practical impossibility of his trying to defeat conclusively the rest of Europe, he lost his appetite for war. He hoped for little more than to enjoy the peace that he had bought at such a steep price at Ryswick. The death of King Charles II of Spain, however, shattered that hope.

For forty years, the European powers had been waiting for the demise of that pitiful example of the results of royal inbreeding. The Spanish king, who was only forty years old at the time of his death, was already decrepit. His deformed "Hapsburg" mouth kept him from chewing his food properly—hence, he had chronic indigestion—and from speaking distinctly. He was constantly sick of some fever or other, had epileptic fits, and in his last years was afflicted with dropsy. His mind was the victim of morbid superstitions, and he lived in perpetual semidarkness in the already gloomy enough Escorial Palace outside Madrid. The only surprise about his death was that it had not come earlier.

For all the apparent weakness of Charles II's mind and his extremely limited knowledge—he did not know, for example, whether such an important fortress as Mons, near Brussels, was in his domains or not—he was a loyal Spaniard. He could not bear to think that at his death without children the enormous empire Spain possessed would be divided among his several relatives in the ruling houses of Europe, all of whom could hardly wait to get their hands on it. He wished to leave the empire intact to the Spanish people.

That empire, the vastest that the modern world had ever known, consisted of Spain itself and the Balearic Islands; over half of Italy (Milan, Naples and Sicily, Sardinia); the Spanish Netherlands (modern Belgium); Mexico; all of Central and South America except Brazil, which was Portuguese; about half the islands of the West Indies, including Cuba; the Philippine Islands; Morocco; and the Canary Islands. The fact that this empire had been mismanaged for over a century only whetted the appetite of monarchs who knew that they could improve the extraction of fabulous revenues from any part that might fall to their inheritance.

All the rulers of Europe expected that the Spanish empire would be divided among the relatives of Charles II.* Of these

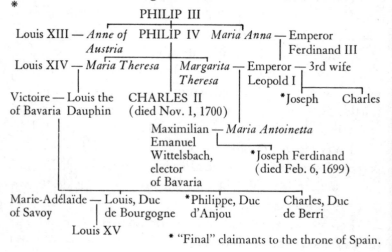

* "Final" claimants to the throne of Spain.

the strongest claimants were Louis XIV himself, by virtue of his Spanish mother (Charles II's aunt) and his Spanish wife (Charles II's older sister); Louis's son and grandsons, by virtue of the fact that Maria Theresa's renunciation of her right to the Spanish throne had never been paid for; the Emperor Leopold I's sons, by virtue of their mother being a younger sister of Charles II and their grandmother having been his aunt. The king of Portugal also asserted a claim, but it was a very weak one legally.

Whoever of these claimants got the throne of Spain itself would upset the balance of power in Europe by linking Spain to his own domain. Consequently, there were many treaties, and also secret agreements which were actually bargains, over what other parts of Spanish lands in Europe would or would not go with the throne. It was conceded that the candidate least dangerous to the balance of power was little Joseph Ferdinand of Bavaria, Emperor Leopold I's grandson and Charles II's great-nephew. But this eight-year-old child upset the diplomatic applecart by inconsiderately dying on February 6, 1699, while Charles II was still alive.

The principal claimants thereafter were Louis XIV (the stronger) and Leopold I. Since these men already occupied thrones, it was inconceivable to other heads of state, especially William III of England, that either should increase his power by annexing Spain to his realm. Since Louis XIV's son (Louis the Dauphin) would presumably inherit the throne of France, he, too, was ruled out by the various treaties. So was the dauphin's oldest son, who would also inherit the French crown. The choice, therefore, was between Louis XIV's second oldest grandson, Philippe, Duc d'Anjou, and Leopold I's younger son, the Archduke Charles (Hapsburg).

Louis XIV had once dreamed of placing a Bourbon on the throne of Spain and, by dint of that, on the throne of the Holy

Roman Empire as well. By 1699, however, he knew that the
rest of Europe would never permit him to extend his dynastic
power to such a degree. He had no wish for another war
against so mighty a coalition of powers as had opposed him only
two years earlier. He was, therefore, willing to settle for what
he could get, and that was to put his grandson on the Spanish
throne.

To that end, Louis XIV sent a wily ambassador, the Marquis d'Harcourt, to Madrid. Harcourt's charm so softened up
the Spanish grandees that the ambassador converted them to
the idea of preferring a French (Bourbon) king to an Austrian
(Hapsburg) one. Leopold I had mistakenly believed that
those nobles would necessarily influence the dimwitted Charles
II of Spain in favor of the Archduke Charles because Spain and
France had been traditional enemies for nearly two hundred
years.

Louis XIV also kept his armies, which he had not demobilized after Ryswick, on the frontiers. They were ready to
support his grandson's claim or confront Leopold I's opposition
to it.

The agony of decision as to which of the candidates—
French or Austrian—he should prefer gave Charles II an
epileptic fit so severe that he knew that even he could not fully
recover from it. On October 2, 1700, he signed his final will,
bequeathing his crown and all his possessions to Philippe, Duc
d'Anjou, and after him to his younger brother Charles, Duc
de Berri (Louis XIV's grandsons), and only thirdly to the
Archduke Charles (Leopold I's younger son). This will, the
result of pressure upon the dying king from his nobles and
also of the pope's advice, was kept so secret that the Austrian
ambassador did not know about it until at the council meeting
immediately following Charles II's death, the chancellor of
Spain bade him a polite adieu.

"Thus," as Voltaire wrote, "after two hundred years of wars and negotiations over certain frontiers of the Spanish States, the House of Bourbon, by one stroke of the pen, obtained the whole empire, without either treaty or intrigue...."

The news of Charles II's death and of his will did not reach Louis XIV until November 8, 1700, one week after the event. At first, the Sun King was in as great a quandary over accepting the bequest for his grandson as his dreary Spanish cousin had been over making it. Perhaps it would be better, Louis thought then, for him to stick to the treaty endorsed by William III and the United Provinces on March 13, 1700, by which the Archduke Charles was to get Spain and the Spanish Netherlands, while the French dauphin got Lorraine and the Italian possessions of Spain. If Louis abided by that treaty, he would have two powerful nations (England and Holland) sworn to support that rich inheritance. If, on the other hand, he accepted the entire Spanish Empire for the Duc d'Anjou, he might well have the same nations—and the Emperor Leopold I as well—his enemies again.

For two days, Louis XIV and his council debated the alternatives in Mme de Maintenon's rooms at Fontainebleau, where the court had gone for the autumn hunting. Foreign Minister Torcy, son of Colbert de Croissy and son-in-law of Pomponne, made the astute observation that even if Louis did abide by the treaty of March 13, 1700 (the Second Partition Treaty), he would have to go to war anyway in order to protect the dauphin's inheritance. Better have Spain as an ally than as an enemy.

The dauphin himself, usually indifferent to matters of state, spoke out strongly in favor of accepting his son's legacy of the twenty-two crowns belonging to the Spanish Empire. Louis XIV, however, maintained that he should not break his word as given in the Second Partition Treaty.

Finally, for the first and only time in his life, Louis XIV consulted a woman's opinion on a matter of government policy. Mme de Maintenon—she was never publicly, or even at court, acknowledged as his wife or as queen—timidly said that she thought the inheritance should be accepted. Louis then dismissed the council.

As Louis left the meeting, he asked one of the court duchesses: "What side are you on?" Then, without waiting for her reply, he added: "Whatever side I take, I know I shall be blamed for what happens."

Louis made his own decision alone. It was, as might have been expected, in favor of accepting the inheritance for Philippe d'Anjou, especially as Charles II's will seemed to express the wishes of the Spanish people. Louis let only a few persons— the Spanish ambassador among them—know what he had decided.

On November 15, the court returned to Versailles. The following day, the Spanish ambassador, the Marquis del Castel dos Rios, presented Louis XIV with letters declaring the eagerness with which the Spaniards awaited the arrival of their new king. Louis, who had previously stationed his seventeen-year-old grandson in an adjoining room, now called the boy into his cabinet.

"Here," Louis said, "is the king for whom Spain calls."

The ambassador knelt before the youth and kissed his hand.

In an unprecedented departure from protocol, both panels of the double door to the king's chamber were now thrown open. The courtiers were called inside.

In a loud voice, Louis XIV proclaimed: "Recognize the Duc d'Anjou as King of Spain. Birth has called him to this crown, and the late king also by his will. The whole Spanish nation desires to have him and asks me to let him go. It is the will of Heaven, and I gladly obey."

Then the Sun King turned to his grandson. "Be a good Spaniard," he admonished him. "That is your first duty now. But never forget that you were born a Frenchman, and foster the unity between our two nations. That is the way to make them happy and to preserve the peace of Europe."

Louis XIV, the greatest royal actor in Europe, had pulled off a scene worthy of its greatest monarch. His *gloire* was at its zenith again as he, the arbiter of nations, handed to the world's largest empire its new sovereign.

As he kissed the Sun King's hand, the Spanish ambassador declared with joy: "The Pyrenees no longer exist. You have leveled them, and we are one."

But as the courtiers heaped congratulations on the new sovereign, and his two brothers kissed him with tears in their eyes, the old monarch doubtless reflected that the Pyrenees still loomed very high indeed, and that his advice to young King Philip V of Spain on preserving the peace of Europe was no magic formula.

For the next two and a half weeks, Louis XIV tried to cram all that he had learned in forty years of experience as an absolute monarch into the comprehension of the young Philip V of Spain. The youth was a good-looking, serious, prudent, and reticent boy who, like many another "middle" son, had lived under the subjection, and perhaps the fear, of his grandfather, his father, and his older brother. He was known as the peacemaker of the family, and his two brothers were fond of him.

Louis XIV now treated Philippe as a fellow monarch on a visit to Versailles, inviting him to his table and addressing him as "Majesty." Philippe, however, was not intelligent enough to absorb more than the drift of Louis's patient advice, and Louis worried about him before the boy set out for Madrid on December 4 after a brilliant farewell party and the shedding of many tears as he entered his coach.

"Never form an attachment to anyone," were Louis's last words to the young king who was to cause him so much woe.

The tears at parting were probably shed out of genuine emotion. Death, of course, had deprived the royal family of France of some members, for even Louis XIV was powerless against that force. This, however, was the only time that any of his dear ones had left Versailles forever by his own inclination—or, to be more exact, by the decision of the king. At the age of sixty-two years, Louis XIV felt the first pangs of the deprivations that are the penalties of longevity.

On August 6, 1682, not only the Sun King himself but all his court had gone wild with joy when the dauphin's wife gave birth to Louis's first grandchild, a son who would presumably assure the Bourbon succession to the throne of France for ages to come. The exuberant grandfather, then at the height of his political power, felt that he had triumphed over nature itself. He allowed everyone at court to give him a congratulatory kiss and permitted the courtiers to carry him on their shoulders from the birth room to his chambers. The baby was named Louis and was given the title of Duc de Bourgogne. Unfortunately, he grew up to be sickly and misshapen.

The infant's father, then aged twenty-one, had proved a disappointment. Blond, fat, and stupid, he had been crushed in spirit by his tutors, who had treated him brutally. After the dauphin was free of them, he never read anything except the birth, marriage, and death notices in the *Gazette*. Hence, he was an expert on genealogy, the only subject he cared to discuss. Sent by his father to command an army besieging a town, "Monseigneur," as the dauphin was called, merely went on long horseback rides. He lived in mortal dread of his father and appealed to Mme de Maintenon to intercede for him with the king whenever he felt he had displeased the sovereign again.

The dauphin's marriage to the physically unattractive Princesse Victoire of Bavaria was unhappy. It was she, however, who disliked him; the heir to the throne found ugly women alluring. She also hated Mme de Maintenon, the profligate life of the court, and the French in general. Louis XIV had small use for her because she would not flatter him. After giving birth to two more sons—Philippe d'Anjou (now King Philip V of Spain) and Charles, Duc de Berri—she died at an early age on April 20, 1690.

Monseigneur consoled himself with another ugly woman, Mlle de Choin, whom he married secretly in 1694 and who never appeared at court.

The dauphin, however, had a love for the arts, particularly music and painting. He would go to the opera in Paris two or three times a week and also amuse himself by rummaging in the antique shops of the capital. His collection of fine furniture, bibelots, and pictures brought so many curious spectators to his apartments at Versailles that he had to arrange a set of secret rooms for himself in order to have any privacy. No one expected much of him, yet everyone fawned on him in preparation for the time that he would be king and could reward them.

Age, and the serious operation he underwent in 1686, had reduced Louis XIV's physical activity. He now followed the hunts in a carriage and took his "walks" in the gardens of Versailles by means of a chair mounted on a three-wheeled platform. The court reflected his inactivity and also his scrupulous attention to religious rituals. Observance of church festivals, fast days, and sanctimonious ceremonies replaced with a pious atmosphere the carefree, sportive days of Versailles when it was new. There were, of course, parties and entertainments, but they had become dull and formal, and during the hard years of the War of the League of Augsburg they grew fewer and less lavish.

The one bright spot in the attenuated gaiety of the court was the arrival of the eleven-year-old Princesse Marie-Adélaïde of Savoy in November, 1697, to be the bride of Louis's eldest grandson, the hunchbacked Duc de Bourgogne. She was like a new child in the family; indeed, since she had the good sense early to ingratiate herself with Mme de Maintenon, the king's wife undertook her education and treated the beautiful little black-eyed girl as her own daughter. Marie-Adélaïde called her "Auntie." Louis himself adored her and allowed her liberties and a familiarity with him that scandalized the older courtiers. Her sister, Marie-Louise of Savoy, married Philip V of Spain, who became a virtual slave to his affection for her.

Mme de Maintenon's major interest, aside from pleasing Louis XIV, was the school for young ladies of the provincial nobility which Louis established for her in 1686 at Saint-Cyr near Versailles. It was not to be a convent—Françoise d'Aubigné had married the crippled Scarron to avoid being confined in one—but it was to have an atmosphere of "civilized piety."

The king, who took a great interest in the students, insisted that their school uniform be quite different from a nun's robes, and that they were to learn beauty secrets and always to be as attractive as possible. He often visited the school, whose headmistress wrote the words of "God Save the King" for her girls to sing to him (the tune, the same as that of "America," is said to be by Lully). At Saint-Cyr, Louis could forget the troubles his politics had brought upon him; he often took along on his visits to the school his cousin, the deposed James II, to watch the girls perform *Esther* or *Athalie*, the two masterful dramas on biblical themes that Racine wrote for them at Mme de Maintenon's request. She did not want her girls playing the passionate heroines of Racine's more typical tragedies.

Unfortunately, Mme de Maintenon's ever-increasing piety induced her to allow this liberal academy to become practically a convent for the students who did not leave it to marry. The buildings subsequently housed the principal French military academy, but were destroyed during World War II.

After the revocation of the Edict of Nantes, of which Mme de Maintenon approved but which she probably did not influence Louis XIV to effect, she wrote: "The king is beginning to think seriously of his salvation. If God preserves him, there will be only one religion in his realm." Perhaps she had in mind the Jansenists as much as the Huguenots. Certainly Louis disliked the Jansenists, who claimed to be good Roman Catholics, as much as he did the Protestants, who definitely were not, even after they had been forced or bribed into conversion to Catholicism.

The Jansenists subscribed to the doctrines of the Flemish bishop Cornelius Jansen. Those were close to Calvinism in that they maintained that salvation is the result of God's grace rather than attainable by "good works" (devotions, confession, penance, etc.). Hence, Jansenists stressed extreme moral uprightness and self-denial, which they believed were a visible sign that God might possibly have destined an individual for His Heaven. Obviously, therefore, the Jansenists disapproved of and deplored the king's disorderly private life.

The Jansenists' austere doctrine impressed many of the leading intellectuals of the seventeenth century, including the

Jacques Bénigne Bossuet (1627–1704), by Hyacinthe Rigaud.

great mathematician and philosopher Blaise Pascal, and Racine, as well as the eloquent preacher Bossuet. Nevertheless, two popes condemned Jansenism.

The stinging chronicler Saint-Simon said of the king that Louis XIV "always pampered himself by making someone else do penance for his sins, and especially the Huguenots and the Jansenists." Having made the Huguenots expiate some of his sins, Louis now began to persecute the Jansenists for the rest of them. The Jansenists operated from two abbeys: Port-Royal in Paris, and the older Port-Royal des Champs in the country. Louis thought these groups capable of causing a division in the one religion which he believed necessary for peace and order in his government.

The harassment of the nuns of Port-Royal began about 1679, when Louis XIV exiled their leader. The convent was then forbidden to accept novices; hence, it was doomed to extinction. Any further persecution of the Jansenists was, therefore, pointless. Louis, however, persisted on the grounds that the convent was a hotbed of the republican sentiments he hated, for Jansenism somewhat stressed the independence of the individual.

Louis was also bored by what he called "the [Jansenists'] long disputes on grace, knowledge of which is not essential for salvation." He was afraid of the influence of the Jansenists for another reason, namely, that their theology appealed particularly to the lawyers of Parlement, whom the king had long distrusted as threats to his autocracy.

Later, under the influence of his stern Jesuit confessor, Père Michel Le Tellier, who had succeeded the tolerant Père La Chaise, Louis extracted a bull from Pope Clement XI decreeing the abolition of Port-Royal. The twenty-two remaining nuns were put out, and the buildings of Port-Royal des Champs were razed in 1710.*

These concerns of the monarch with religion were a kind of superstitious down payment for the divine protection and aid he knew he would need in the war that was about to engulf him.

Although the maritime powers of England and Holland recognized Philip V as the legitimate king of Spain, Emperor Leopold I refused to do so. Leopold believed that he and his

---

* The buildings of Port-Royal in Paris are now part of the maternity hospital at 119 Boulevard du Port-Royal. The somewhat restored ruins of Port-Royal des Champs, which contain interesting relics of the Jansenists, can be seen about four miles northwest of St.-Remy-les-Chevreuse, some twenty miles southwest of Paris.

sons had been illegally excluded from their inheritance. For a time, however, it seemed that there might nevertheless be peace. No one could believe that Leopold would go to war without allies, and Louis had bribed the English Parliament into a pacifistic attitude.

In the spring and early summer of 1701, however, Louis's efforts to support and protect his grandson-king were, perhaps deliberately, misinterpreted in England by William III and his party in Parliament. The previously antiwar Parliament instructed William to seek allies in order to check the apparently inevitable union of France and the Spanish Empire. Consequently, William III negotiated another Grand Alliance (England, Holland, the Empire, and Brandenburg) at The Hague on August 31, 1701. The terms of this alliance, principally the eternal separation of the French and Spanish crowns, were sent to Louis XIV, who interpreted them correctly as an act of war.

Still, the terms could have been compromised. On September 6, 1701, however, the former King James II of England died at Saint-Germain. His widow, whose marriage to James Louis XIV had maliciously arranged, besought Louis with much weeping to recognize her oldest son as King James III, the rightful heir to the English throne. Foolishly Louis did so.

This towering blunder, a direct insult to William III and to the English, who had recently excluded the Catholic branch of the Stuart family forever from the succession, was as good as a declaration of war by France on England. The only possible excuse for Louis's rash act is his chivalrous respect for the "divine right" of kings, which the democratic English had long before listed among backward superstitions—like chivalry itself.

Before hostilities commenced—although Emperor Leopold had begun a private campaign in Italy—William III died, on

March 8, 1702. Anne, James II's second daughter by his first and Protestant wife, succeeded him. A stupid woman, she was completely under the thumb of Sarah Churchill, whose husband, John Churchill, Duke of Marlborough, was the real ruler of England in his capacity of England's great general.

Marlborough had learned the art of war under Turenne as a volunteer cadet in the Dutch war of the 1670's. One of Turenne's principles, that "in the end, the army must fight," became "Handsome Jack" Churchill's also. He seems to have passed it on to his descendant, England's leader in World War II, Winston Churchill. No matter what happened, Malbrouck,* as the French called him, was cool-headed, a factor that made him supreme in field battles. He was also a shrewd diplomatist.

The Emperor Leopold's general, almost as brilliant a military leader as Marlborough, was Prince Eugene of Savoy, son of the Olympe Mancini whom the young Louis XIV had once admired. Louis had turned against Olympe because of her involvement in a scandal centering around a woman, La Voisin, who sold love potions and possibly poisons to his court ladies. Eugene, in revenge, and also because Louis disapproved of his morals, left France and devoted his military genius to Louis's enemy, Leopold I.

Against these accomplished strategists, who always agreed with each other, Louis XIV placed at the head of his army Louis Joseph, Duc de Vendôme, a grandson of Henry IV. He was also the son of a Mancini girl and so Prince Eugene's cousin. Similarly, another of Louis's generals, James Fitzjames (Stuart), Duke of Berwick, an illegitimate son of James II, was Marlborough's nephew. The war was, in a minor sense, a family feud.

* The well-known French song, *Malbrouck s'en va t'en guerre* ("Marlborough Is Off to War") originated at this time and became the most popular song of those war days. Ironically, its tune is English—the same as "For He's a Jolly Good Fellow."

These French generals and two others, Claude de Villars and François de Villeroi, son of Louis's old tutor "Monsieur Ouisire," were not the best to take the field against Marlborough and Eugene. Vendôme was vain, lazy, and careless of detail; Berwick was sluggish; Villars was competent, but in strategy little more than a ruthless plunderer; Villeroi was almost incompetent and allowed himself to be captured. Louis XIV's war minister Chamillart was not the man Louvois had been or even Barbézieux; he had great power—both the war and the treasury departments—but he could succeed only in remedying defeats, not in achieving victories.

France not only had mediocre generals but was not in good condition for a war in which it would have to fight virtually alone on four fronts—Flanders, Germany, Italy, Spain—against the rest of Europe. Neither the army nor the treasury had completely recovered from the last war, only five years previously. About half of the 200,000 men in the French army were raw recruits, poorly trained and equipped. The Spanish alliance was more a liability than an asset.

On May 15, 1702, England, Holland, and the Empire officially declared war. The conflict, known as the War of the Spanish Succession, began with some successes for the French. In spite of reversals in Italy and Spain, and the desertion of some of France's allies, the French made steady gains in the northern and eastern theaters of the war, and by early 1704 were threatening the emperor's capital of Vienna.

Marlborough, whose activities had been hampered by his Dutch allies, determined to rescue his more strategically helpful ally Emperor Leopold I. Being his own war minister and also in control of Queen Anne, the English Parliament, and the English treasury, the duke needed to feel no responsibility to anyone but himself and to nothing but his own resourcefulness. Therefore, he led his army to the Danube to join Prince

Eugene's and smash the French forces, which were far from their bases of supply and would be hard to reinforce from home.

Louis XIV made the mistake of recalling Villars from the Danube and replacing him with the dull Comte Ferdinand de Marsin, whom the religious faction at Versailles seems to have imposed upon the king. As in the previous war, Louis was directing the campaigns by correspondence from Versailles, and Chamillart was merely effecting the king's orders. Either Marsin was too unimaginative to guess, or Louis was too far from the front to anticipate, that Marlborough and Eugene intended to attack the overextended French army.

That, however, was just what the two superior strategists did, and inflicted a terrible defeat on the French at Blenheim on August 13, 1704. Marsin's army of 60,000 men lost 40,000 in contrast to the Anglo-Imperial losses of about 5,000 out of 50,000. The French army was thus rendered incapable of action. It was the first serious disaster to the French military machine since Louis XIV and the Le Telliers had set it in motion forty years earlier. The French felt so humiliated that they still refer to the engagement as the Battle of Hochstadt in order to disclaim association with one of the greatest of England's victories.

The English rewarded their fighting duke with the splendid palace of Blenheim, near Oxford, still the seat of the dukes of Marlborough. The emperor made him a prince of the Empire with the domain of Mindelheim.

At Versailles, however, no one dared tell the Sun King of the disaster at Blenheim. Finally, Mme de Maintenon suggested to him that he might no longer be invincible. Louis's spirits fell. He believed that God had forsaken him, and he wept at the thought that the defeat might be divine punishment on him for his sins.

The French people grew more and more alarmed as reports of the defeat reached them. They blamed Louis for it, and deeply resented the celebration he ordered for the birth of his first great-grandson. (Named Louis, the infant died four months later.) Morale was gone, for reports of other losses had preceded or immediately followed the dire news of Blenheim.

The English had captured Gibraltar on August 4, 1704, thus gaining control of the Mediterranean. In Spain, where Queen Anne was supporting the Austrian Archduke Charles's claim to the throne occupied by Philip V, the English captured the vital cities of Valencia and Barcelona and overran Catalonia. Then, in March, 1705, they annihilated the French fleet off Malaga. The French navy was thereafter back where it was before Louis XIV, aided by Colbert, had developed it to peak efficiency.

To prevent an invasion of their country by Marlborough, the French now had to fight a defensive war on a long, crescent-shaped frontier that stretched from the English Channel to Switzerland. Louis soothed Villars's injured feelings with the title of duke and recalled him to command that front. Both the king and his general were unaware that Marlborough's allies were refusing to let him risk another Blenheim, and Louis regarded Marlborough's failure to attack as an answer to his constant prayers that the English duke would not do so. Villars and Marlborough exchanged compliments and gifts while each strengthened his position throughout 1705.

In May of 1706, Villeroi, who had replaced Villars on the Flemish front, tired of being criticized by Louis XIV for his purely defensive campaign. Preparing to attack Marlborough, he divided his forces in such a way that Marlborough saw a chance to break through them and immediately grasped it. Villeroi marched to meet him in open battle and fell a victim to Marlborough's superior skill on the field of Ramillies on May

23. The French were completely routed, losing 20,000 men, mostly through capture. They also lost complete control of Flanders, which Marlborough overran. He even besieged the town of Menin, which was just within the boundary of France.

Villeroi waited a week before he dared report the disaster of Ramillies in person to the king. Louis XIV, however, merely said to the sixty-year-old general: "Sir, we are just not lucky at our age."

In Spain, an Anglo-Portuguese army—Portugal had deserted France as an ally—invaded the capital of Madrid and proclaimed the Archduke Charles king of Spain on June 25, 1706.

Attempting to repair the damage he had suffered in Flanders, Louis XIV transferred the Duc de Vendôme from Italy to that area. This move, however, left the Italian front vulnerable and permitted Prince Eugene to capture the vital city of Turin on September 7, 1706. That loss, the result of poor directives from the behind-the-lines administrators in Versailles, threw panic into the French forces. They retreated in disorder, leaving Italy in the hands of the Imperials.

In desperation, Louis XIV renewed the negotiations for peace that he had begun in 1705. He even offered to rescind his acceptance of Charles II of Spain's will. The members of the Grand Alliance, however, each of whom had his own conditions for peace and all of whom were flushed with success, made such impossible terms that Louis XIV was forced to continue his war of endurance.

In early 1707, the tide turned for France. The Spanish were enraged by the imposition on them of the Archduke Charles as king in defiance of Charles II's wishes. They rose against the Portuguese, who had installed the archduke, and threw him out. On April 25, 1707, the duke of Berwick defeated the Anglo-Portuguese army at Almanza. That victory

saved Spain for Philip V—and Louis XIV. Berwick sub-
sequently cleared Louis's and Philip's enemies out of Spain.

This success was followed by a victory by Villars in Germany on May 23, 1707; and, on August 22, by the defeat of
Prince Eugene, who was besieging the vital Mediterranean
port of Toulon in French territory. Villeroi was holding the
Flemish front secure. But Italy remained lost, and Louis XIV
withdrew his forces from the peninsula.

In behalf of the Old Pretender, Louis, in March, 1708,
mounted a naval expedition against England via Scotland.
The Scots, he believed, would rise to restore James III, whom
they regarded as their own king because he was descended
from the old Scottish royal family. The invasion stood a chance
of success, for England's troops were engaged on the Continent.
But the English war ministry quickly recalled a dozen bat-
talions and arrested the leaders of the Scots, who would have
helped the prince land. Learning of this turn of events, the
expedition's admiral just sailed his ships back home.

France's continental sucesses during 1707 induced Vendôme
to attempt to break Marlborough's lines of communication in
Flanders. Louis XIV backed him in this plan because it
offered his grandson, the Duc de Bourgogne, who was nom-
inally in command of the army, a chance for *gloire*. But that
heir to the throne had been taught by Fénelon to believe that
war is a lamentable necessity of politics rather than a source
of glory, and he argued with the actual commander, the old
warhorse Vendôme.

The result of their disputes was defeat at Oudenarde on
July 11, 1708. This was followed by a retreat so poorly managed
that, on December 9, Marlborough and Eugene were able to
capture the supposedly impregnable fortress of Lille after a
siege of nearly four months.

The Duc de Vendôme and the Duc de Bourgogne blamed

each other for these disasters, which opened a way for an invasion of France and an attack on Paris itself. A Dutch detachment actually reached Versailles and kidnapped a courtier, thinking that he was the dauphin. Pope Clement XI, however, dissuaded the emperor—now Joseph I, Leopold having died on May 5, 1705—from pursuing his advantage. The pope was on the side of Philip V, if not exactly on France's side.

The religious faction in the court blamed Vendôme for the defeat at Oudenarde. Characteristic of the way in which the courtiers aped their monarch's excessive and superficial piety, one remarked to the venerable veteran that his reverses were due to his failure to attend mass regularly.

"I suppose you think," Vendôme replied, "that the Protestant Marlborough goes to mass more often than I do."

Naturally, the experienced military officers took Vendôme's side. So did the people. The dissension infected the whole nation.

Then came the terrible winter of 1708–9, which killed men, farm animals, fruit and olive trees and grapevines, and froze the wheat seeds in the earth. A shortage of bread in Paris drove the women to march on Versailles to demand help from the king. Louis had his bodyguard turn them away. Starvation elsewhere produced crimes, suicides, and obscenities. The currency fell to one-third of its value. The soldiers were unpaid. There was no money to import wheat. Rich people, including Louis XIV himself, sold their silverware for cash to buy food. The irreverent made a shocking parody of the Lord's Prayer:

> Our Father which art at Versailles, thy name is hallowed no more, thy kingdom is great no more, thy will is no longer done on earth or on the seas. Give us this day the bread we lack. . . .

Louis XIV was ready to make almost any concession in

the peace conference he had been forced to request in The Hague. The Dutch, who spoke for the entire alliance, demanded even more concessions. Their ultimatum was that Louis surrender all the conquests he had made in Germany during the past fifty years and hand over several French towns on the frontier. The Dutch went too far, however, in demanding that Louis personally see to the expulsion of Philip V from Spain within two months.

Louis XIV balked. He referred the matter to his people by means of propagandistic letters to the royal representatives in the provinces. The French boiled with indignation at the insufferable terms the Dutch demanded for peace and urged their king to reject them.

With that mandate from his people, Louis XIV again prepared a campaign against Marlborough and Eugene in Flanders. Vendôme having been disgraced by the calamity of Oudenarde and the loss of Lille, Louis XIV replaced him with Villars, the only one of his generals who had not yet lost a battle throughout the seven years of the war.

Villars proposed to risk a battle with his opponents, able though he knew they were in field maneuvers. They were also unwilling to hazard an encounter. Nevertheless, Villars got Louis XIV's permission to force a battle on them by reasoning that it was the only way to take the pressure off his army. It was a great risk, as Villars's was the only army capable of an offensive that was left to France. It could not be replaced since France was bankrupt of money, supplies, and men.

The two forces met at Malplaquet near Mons on September 11, 1710—80,000 allied troops against Villars's 70,000. Villars received a wound that kept him from leading his division, and the French were compelled to withdraw at a moment when they might have won the day.

Actually the Battle of Malplaquet could be called a draw, for the allies lost more men than the French. Thirty thousand corpses lay on the field, and the blood upon it was ankle-deep. Marlborough dared not risk another engagement, and the French spent the rest of the year in a successful defensive campaign.

The carnage at Malplaquet sickened the English, and in 1711 they voted the Whig war party out of power. Shortly thereafter, Emperor Joseph I died. His brother, the Archduke Charles, had to abandon the campaign in Spain to claim the succession to the throne of the Empire, thus ensuring Philip V's success in retaining his throne. Prince Eugene had to withdraw his army to Vienna in order to guarantee the archduke's being elected Emperor Charles VI against French pressure on the Imperial Electors. Marlborough, who had now lost control of English policy—his wife had also lost favor with Queen Anne—stood alone.

England no more wanted Emperor Charles in control of Austria and Spain than it wanted Louis XIV dominating Spain through his grandson. The English Tory party wanted peace anyway. England and France, therefore, began peace talks in July and came to terms on October 8, 1711. The other members of the alliance, dismayed and disgusted by England's withdrawal from the war, agreed to a peace conference with France at Utrecht in January, 1712.

Emperor Charles VI, however, still held out, but his general, Prince Eugene, suffered a smashing defeat at Denain on July 24, 1712, at the hands of Villars. That resounding victory for the French saved France at the conference table. The Dutch, under pressure from the English, had to modify their demands, for the Battle of Denain had destroyed their lines of communication with the Imperial forces, and they could not fight alone. Marlborough had been recalled, to be charged with corruption* and cowardice by the Tories.

The treaty of Utrecht, signed on April 11, 1713, gave Louis XIV the prize for which the entire war had been fought, namely, universal recognition of his grandson as King Philip V of Spain. Philip, however, relinquished all claim to the French crown. Louis paid for this objective by yielding the Spanish Netherlands to the Dutch, who would transfer it to Austria after an agreement had been reached for the protection of this buffer between the United Provinces and France. Hence, the Dutch got what they had been fighting to maintain for forty years. Louis also surrendered to their previous possessors all the territories, except Strasbourg, that he had annexed in the same period. The Spanish possessions in Italy went to Austria.

Villars's victories in the summer of 1713 compelled Emperor Charles VI to ratify the Treaty of Utrecht in a separate treaty with France, signed at Radstadt on March 16, 1714.

The dreadful war was over at last, but the settlement only provided for another one. Austria, now in possession of Flanders and most of Italy, was as much a threat to England as France had been. The recognition of the elector of Brandenburg as king of Prussia, and the existence of that kingdom, prepared the way for the elector's son, Frederick the Great, to challenge both Austria and England. In America, where the war had been known as Queen Anne's War, the shift in colonial territory between England and France was to produce tensions culminating in the bloody French and Indian War.

The valiant spirit of the French that had rallied to their monarch when his back was to the wall remained, but France had lost to England the political domination of Europe.

---

*Louis XIV had attempted to bribe Marlborough with two million livres ($5,000,000) but withdrew the offer after Denain.

IX

THE SUN SETS

Politically, France had been humbled by the powers that Louis XIV had once bent to his will. Culturally, the spirit of the Age of Louis XIV had all but obliterated national trends. England was the one nation least affected, but even in that seagirt realm, French styles in art, dress, and decoration had made themselves felt. The upper strata of English society retained their own language; elsewhere, French had become the universal tongue of the upper classes to such a degree that educated people scarcely used their national tongue. International documents were now written in French instead of in Latin, which Louis XIV had labored in his youth to learn in order that he might completely understand their implications.

The nation that all others imitated was itself, however, in sad straits. In 1707, Vauban, the great military engineer, then seventy-four years old, published a little book on the need for tax reform in France. "Nearly a tenth of the people," Vauban wrote, "are reduced to beggary, and of the other nine tenths the majority are more in a condition to receive charity than to give it."

Louis XIV considered the work libelous and had it symbolically "punished" as if it were a petty criminal. Within six weeks, Vauban died of the effects of this disgrace.

The cost of the government was four times greater than its income. The deficit was made up by loans which amounted to a colossal indebtedness. Much of this borrowed money came from private individuals like the banker Samuel Bernard, a Rothschild or a Morgan ahead of his time, or from the Paris Brothers, who underwrote the cost of Villars's expedition that culminated in the victory at Denain.

Financial assistance from these industrialists naturally raised their class into a position from which it could dictate to the government. On the other hand, taxes so burdened the peasantry that many farmers turned to industry, and French agriculture suffered in consequence. This shift of labor produced a working class large and strong enough to dictate to factory owners. Such changes were almost imperceptibly sapping the former vigor of Louis XIV's autocracy. The French people were making themselves heard.

*Télémaque,** the narrative that Fénelon composed for the moral instruction of the dauphin's son, was published without the author's consent in 1699. It soon became one of the most widely read, hence influential, books of modern times. Fénalon's message can be abstracted in such modern-sounding sentiments from *Télémaque* as:

> The human race is one family. . . . Nations henceforth will be one people. . . . All peoples are brothers. . . . War is the shame of the human race. . . . Whoever prefers his own glory to human feelings is a monster. . . . Absolute power reduces all subject to it to the level of slaves. . . . Tyranny perishes through its

---

* The original title was *Suite de l'Odicée d'Homère* (A Sequel to Homer's Odyssey). It deals with the adventures of Telemachus, the son of Odysseus.

Louis XIV about 1714, wax portrait with real hair by Benoist. Versailles.

own excessiveness and by revolt, for its strength does not come from the love or consent of the people.

All readers of *Télémaque* could see through the veil of its mythology to Louis XIV and his absolutism. The king, of course, had the book suppressed, and punished its printer. It was reissued in Holland, however, and was widely circulated from there. The author, being archbishop of Cambrai, was beyond the reach of royal admonition.

Revolts of oppressed peasants and rebellions of persecuted religious minorities caused cracks in the foundation of Louis XIV's system more noticeable than the shift in the social structure or the murmurs of criticism like Fénelon's. Antoine Watteau, the great painter of the last years of Louis XIV's reign, summed up the tone of the period in his masterpiece *The Embarcation for Cythera*, now in the Louvre, Paris. The canvas shows a group of elegant courtiers wistfully boarding a boat that will transport them to a distant isle quite out of the real world, where they will live as gorgeous ghosts of an era fading into the autumn twilight they leave behind them.

The aged monarch disdained to notice the cracks and fissures. At the age of seventy-five he was in good general health and had lost none of his virility. Toothless, and jowled, and white-haired—although he concealed that last betrayal of old age under an enormous black wig—he was still a towering personality. His vigor and courage during the perilous years of the War of the Spanish Succession appear in his forceful, optimistic communications to his generals. He wrote to Villars on the eve of the daring battle of Denain that if the army should be defeated, "I would go to Péronne or St.-Quentin [in Brittany], gather all the troops I might have, make a last effort with you, and we would perish together or save the state."

Perhaps Louis XIV unconsciously desired so heroic a death. Before Villars's victory, a series of tragedies in the royal family had cheated the king of his hopes for a long, unbroken succession of heirs to the throne. On April 16, 1711, the dauphin died of smallpox, unlamented, and so uncared for by the courtiers, who fled from his infected palace at Meudon, that his coffin was made too small and the corpse had to be doubled up to fit into it.

The new direct heir was Louis's grandson Louis, Duc de Bourgogne, for whom Fénelon had written *Télémaque*. The only one of the family with what might be called a public conscience, he was a solemn, withdrawn twenty-nine-year-old with less experience of people as they are than as he found them represented in books. In spite of a certain intelligence, he was, like the rest of the family, essentially humorless. Half the court thought him a coward and a prig. Only the challenge of being king could have proved whether or not he was too philosophical to make decisions or effect the administrative reforms he thought necessary.

The chance was denied him. On February 12, 1712, his vivacious young wife, Marie-Adélaïde, succumbed to "spotted" fever (probably measles or scarlet fever), which the court physicians undoubtedly aggravated with their barbarous remedies. The Duc, who had refused to leave her sickbed, caught the disease and died six days after her. So did their older son, the five-year-old Duc de Bretagne, on March 8.

The Duchesse de Ventadour, governess of their younger son, aged two, saved him from dying of the same infectious malady by refusing to let the doctors treat him. She herself nursed him back to something resembling health. But no one expected that this sickly little Duc d'Anjou would live for sixty-two more years and reign for fifty-nine of them as King Louis XV.

A more likely heir was Charles, Duc de Berri, the younger brother of Philip V of Spain, who had relinquished all claim to the French throne. But Charles died of the effects of a hunting accident on May 4, 1714.

One of Louis XIV's principles of government was that a monarch can control the future by careful planning and by facing problems before they arise. Knowing that his own death would surely occur before his great-grandson was of an age to rule, the king tried to prevent anarchy during the regency that would be necessary by arranging for that body at once. He appointed as actual regent his nephew, the Duc d'Orléans, son of his dead brother Philippe. A council of fourteen, including Louis XIV's now legitimized sons by Mme de Montespan, was to control the regent's decisions by a majority vote.

Those provisions, however, only stirred up trouble and factions—as is inevitable when possible successors to a throne are named before the sovereign himself is defunct. For by legitimizing the Duc du Maine and the Comte de Toulouse, Louis XIV had made them potential heirs to the throne, whereas the Duc d'Orléans considered himself a much nearer and more legal inheritor of the crown. And Philippe d'Orléans, a shrewd politician, was also a dissolute freethinker whom no one trusted.

The last will and testament by which Louis XIV set up this regency—signed and sealed with seven seals on August 27, 1714—as everyone including Louis himself knew, would be only a scrap of paper after he was dead. It was merely a token of his wish to give his people a period of peace in compensation for the deprivation his wars had caused them. Doubt as to the future, therefore, clouded the Sun King's last two years, which had already been darkened by sorrow. At the close of his reign, Louis XIV was as tragic a figure as any of the kings of Racine whose royal manner he had once imitated.

Mme de Maintenon tried to console her troubled husband by surrounding him with the friends of his youth—the widow of his brother Philippe, and Villeroi, who had been brought up with the king. With Louis's favorite child, the responsible and responsive Duc du Maine, they made a convivial three-some. The dowager Duchesse d'Orléans was a talkative old gossip, and Villeroi told stories that reminded them all of the brave days of long ago. Occasionally they made the melancholy monarch smile.

Mme de Maintenon revived the entertainments at court that had languished during the hard years of the war. The parties were smaller than previously, and more informal, and the guests were restricted to those the hostess knew might amuse her husband and share his tastes. She also persuaded Louis to revisit the theater, which he had stopped attending during his period of penitence. Scenes from the Molière comedies he once had loved were staged again at Versailles and at Louis's retreat at Marly. Perhaps the old king watched them pensively, pondering how different his life—and history itself—might have been if he had listened more to Molière's sly exposures of human frailty than to the fanatics he had allowed to counsel him.

In January, 1715, Louis XIV's understanding of European politics led him to attempt to guarantee peace for the future by stronger means than a mere will. Alarmed by the rise in power of England, the new kingdom of Prussia, and Russia, which Peter the Great had made a factor in European politics, Louis planned an alliance among the old powers—France, the Empire, Spain—that might prevent another war like that of the War of the Spanish Succession. He saw that the Hapsburg-Bourbon rivalry was now an anachronism. Could he possibly have foreseen the cataclysms of the next two hundred years caused by the rivalry of those new powers?

Unfortunately, the ambassador who was to carry this proposal to the Emperor Charles VI in Vienna was delayed. Before action could be taken on it, an ugly spot had appeared on Louis XIV's leg. The doctors diagnosed the sore as gangrene—incurable and fatal.

On the following day, August 11, 1715, Louis XIV received a delegate from Parlement. The king was now thin, and shrunken, and had lost his appetite—but not his temper. Thinking the monarch tired and feeble, the magistrate used all his lawyer's wiles to evade Louis's questions and to seem obedient when actually he was defiant.

Like an old lion, Louis roared that he would turn the man out of office, stamped his foot, and smashed his walking stick on a marble table. The representative of Parlement merely smiled ironically and withdrew.

Two days later, the king received an envoy from the governor of a province of Persia. Louis persuaded himself that the man was the ambassador of the shah of Persia himself. The court chamberlain perceived that Louis wished to make the grand gesture of receiving the Persian in state, and so did not reveal the true nature of the emissary's rather insignificant status.

Louis XIV dressed himself for the occasion in black and gold-embroidered velvet, put on his fabulous diamonds, ranged the Duc d'Orléans on one side of him and the five-year-old dauphin on the other, and in spite of the pain in his leg stood erect before his throne in Versailles's grand Hall of Mirrors while the royal drummers beat a long roll of salute to the impostor. It was the last show of magnificence for the Sun King in his enchanted isle of Versailles.

By August 22, Louis was too feeble to review his bodyguard and delegated the honor to his tiny heir. He had begun to use to the child the phrase, "In the days when I was king," as he struggled to impart some of the tricks of ruling he hoped would make the boy's task easier. But, on August 26, the king celebrated the Feast of Saint Louis by dining in the presence of the court to the accompaniment of his beloved violin orchestra. Afterward he fainted and was put to bed for the last time—without the customary long ceremony.

He had been an artist in living, and he was determined to be an artist in dying. The deathbed scenes were worthy of a great dramatist. To his courtiers, the king said:

"Gentlemen, I am satisfied with your services. You have faithfully served me with a desire to please. I am distressed not to have better repaid you. I leave you with regret. Serve the Dauphin with the same affection that you have served me; he is a child of five years who can suffer many vexations, for I recall that I suffered many during my childhood. I am leaving you, but the State will always remain. Be faithfully attached to it and let your example serve all my other subjects. Be united and in accord; this is the unity and strength of the State . . . follow the orders that my nephew gives you; I hope that he will always do good. I hope also that you will do your duty and that you will sometimes recall me to mind."

Then he sent for his great-grandson and delivered his celebrated farewell to the little five-year-old:

"Soon you will be king of a great kingdom. I urge you not to forget your duty to God; remember that you owe everything to Him. Try to remain at peace with your neighbors. I loved war too much. Do not imitate me in that or in overspending. Take advice in everything; try to find the best course and follow it. Lighten your people's burden as soon as possible, and do what I have had the misfortune not to do myself."

By August 30, the king was so far gone that Mme de Maintenon's confessor advised her to leave him alone with the priests and the doctors. She left Versailles forever at four o'clock that afternoon. The other courtiers also left off attending the dying sovereign. The Duc du Maine gave a gay supper party; the Duc d'Orléans plotted his course as the virtual ruler of France.

Louis XIV lingered one more day. Recovering consciousness while receiving the last rites of the Church, he murmured: "Oh, Lord, help me! Hasten to succor me!" Those were his last words. At eight fifteen the following morning, September 1, 1715, Louis XIV ended his turbulent life very quietly.

The king's body was taken to the traditional burial place of French royalty, the Abbey of Saint-Denis, then on the outskirts of Paris. The *De Profundis* which his father, Louis XIII, had composed on his deathbed was chanted at the solemn high funeral mass. But outside the church the people howled with joy, shouted insults at the casket before the high altar, and drank to their deliverance from a man who had visited misery, defeat, and slaughter upon them far too long. None of that impious crowd seemed to recognize that Louis XIV had been the greatest king of French history.

CHRONOLOGY

Days of the month are given "old style" on the premise that such was the actual date on which the event occurred. For "new style" dates, add ten or, in a month of thirty days, eleven.

1638   Louis XIV born, September 5.

1643   Louis XIII dies, May 14.

1648   First War of the Fronde begins, August 26. Peace of Westphalia concludes Thirty Years' War, October 24.

1649   Treaty of Rueil ends First War of the Fronde, April 1.

1650   Second War of the Fronde begins, January 18.

1651   Louis XIV declares his majority, September 7.

1652   Second War of the Fronde ends, October 21.

1654   Coronation of Louis XIV at Rheims, June 7.

1659   Peace of the Pyrenees concluded, November 7. End of love affair between Louis XIV and Marie Mancini.

1660   Louis XIV marries Maria Theresa of Spain, June 9.

1661   Cardinal Mazarin dies, March 9. Louis XIV assumes full monarchical powers. Arrest of Fouquet, September 5. Colbert takes over finance ministry (appointed minister of finance, 1665). The Grand Dauphin born, November 1.

Remodeling of Louis XIII's hunting lodge at Versailles begun.

1664   First great fete at Versailles ("The Pleasures of the Enchanted Isle"), May 7–10.

1665   Philip IV of Spain, Louis XIV's father-in-law, dies, September 17; succeeded by Charles II, his son by his second wife, Marianna of Austria.

1666   Death of Anne of Austria, Louis XIV's mother, January 20.

1667   War of Devolution against Spain begins with Turenne's invasion of the Spanish Netherlands (modern Belgium), May 24.

1668   Franche-Comté conquered by Condé, February 4–13. Treaty of Aix-la-Chapelle ends War of Devolution, May 2. Louis XIV meets Françoise d'Aubigné Scarron (later Mme de Maintenon).

1670   Treaty of Dover allies France with England, June 1.

1672   Dutch War begins, March 28. French army crosses the Rhine, June 12. William of Orange becomes Stadtholder of the United Provinces (modern Holland), July 3.

1677   William of Orange marries Mary Stuart, daughter of the future King James II of England, thus canceling terms of Treaty of Dover and preparing the way for him to become King William III of England.

1678   Treaty of Nijmegen ends Dutch War, August 11.

1680–81   Persecution of Huguenots begins in earnest; the *dragonnade* instituted, March.

1682   Louis XIV makes Versailles the seat of French government, May 6.

1683   Queen Maria Theresa dies, July 30. Colbert dies, September 6. Louis XIV secretly marries Mme de Maintenon, probably on October 9.

1684   Peace of Ratisbon (Regensburg), August.

1685   James II succeeds Charles II as king of England, February 6. Edict of Nantes (1598) revoked by Edict of Fontainebleau, October 18. Mass emigration of Huguenots as persecution of them increases.

1686 League of Augsburg formed, July 9.

1688 James II dethroned as king of England, November 5; escapes to France, January, 1689. Emperor Leopold I subdues Turks, September 6.

1689 William of Orange proclaimed King William III of England, and Mary as joint sovereign, February 13. English Act of Succession bars the Catholic branch of the Stuart family from the English throne forever. Fénelon becomes tutor to Louis XIV's grandson, the Duc de Bourgogne. War of the League of Augsburg begins, September 24. Devastation of Rhenish Palatinate, October 30–June 1, 1690.

1690 Battle of the Boyne and Battle of Beachy Head, July 1.

1697 Treaty of Ryswick ends War of the League of Augsburg, September 11.

1700 Charles II of Spain dies, November 1. Louis XIV proclaims his grandson Philippe, Duc d'Anjou, King Philip V of Spain, November 16.

1701 William III negotiates Grand Alliance, August 31. Dethroned James II dies, September 6; Louis XIV recognizes James II's son as rightful heir to English crown—a virtual declaration of war on England.

1702 William III dies, March 8; succeeded by sister-in-law Anne. Duke of Marlborough the virtual ruler of England. Official declaration of War of the Spanish Succession, May 15.

1704 Marlborough defeats French at Blenheim (Hochstadt), August 13.

1706 Battle of Ramillies, May 23.

1708 Abortive French invasion of England, March. Battle of Oudenarde, July 11.

1709 Terrible winter causes famine and uprisings in France.

1710 Battle of Malplaquet, September 11. Destruction of Port-Royal.

1711 Death of Louis XIV's son, the Grand Dauphin, April 14.

1712 Peace conference begins at Utrecht, January. Deaths of

Duchesse de Bourgogne, February 12; Duc de Bourgogne, February 18; Duc de Bretagne (their older son), March 8. Louis XIV's great-grandson becomes heir to the French throne. Battle of Denain, July 24. Marlborough recalled as English general.

1713   Treaty of Utrecht virtually ends War of Spanish Succession, April 11; confirmed by Treaty of Radstadt, March 16, 1714.

1714   Louis XIV's will, establishing regency for his great-grandson, signed, August 27.

1715   Louis XIV dies, September 1.

BIBLIOGRAPHY

Of the enormous number of works in many languages on Louis XIV and his reign, only recent and easily available works in English are listed below. Excluded also are individual listings of English translations of the many volumes of letters and memoirs which contain details—usually gossipy and inaccurate —of the life and character of personages in the court and of the daily life at Versailles. An admirable compendium of these is Ziegler's *At the Court of Versailles* (see below).

ASHLEY, MAURICE. *Louis XIV and the Greatness of France.* New York: Macmillan (The Free Press), 1965.

DURANT, WILL and ARIEL. *The Age of Louis XIV.* New York: Simon and Schuster, 1963.

ESCHOLIER, MARC. *Port-Royal, the Drama of the Jansenists.* New York: Hawthorn, 1968.

GRAMONT, SANCHE DE, ed. *The Age of Magnificence.* New York: Putnam's, 1963.

LEWIS, WARREN HAMILTON. *Louis XIV, an Informal Portrait.* New York: William Sloane Associates, 1959.

——— *The Splendid Century: Life in the France of Louis XIV.* New York: William Sloane Associates, 1953; Garden City: Doubleday (Anchor Books), 1957.

————— *The Sunset of the Splendid Century: The Life and Times of Louis Auguste de Bourbon, Duc du Maine, 1670–1736*. New York: William Sloane Associates; Garden City: Doubleday (Anchor Books), 1957.

MITFORD, NANCY. *The Sun King*. New York: Viking, 1967.

SAINT-SIMON, LOUIS DE ROUVROY, DUC DE. *Historical Memoirs* (Vol. I, 1691–1709; Vol. II, 1710–1715), edited and translated by Lucy Norton. New York: McGraw-Hill, 1967–68.

TREASURE, GEOFFREY. *Seventeenth-Century France*. New York: Barnes & Noble, 1966; Garden City: Doubleday (Anchor Books), 1967.

VOLTAIRE (FRANÇOIS-MARIE AROUET). *The Age of Louis XIV*, trans. by Martyn F. Pollack. New York: Dutton (Everyman's Library), 1966.

WOLF, JOHN B. *Louis XIV*. New York: Norton, 1968.

ZIEGLER, GILETTE. *At the Court of Versailles: Eyewitness Reports from the Reign of Louis XIV*, trans. by Simon Watson Taylor. New York: Dutton, 1966.

INDEX